Parents on the Team

Parents on the Team

Sara L. Brown
and Martha S. Moersch,
Editors

Ann Arbor
The University of Michigan Press

50309

Library of Congress Cataloging in Publication Data

Main entry under title:

Parents on the team.

    Bibliography: p.
    1.   Handicapped children—Education—Addresses,
essays, lectures.   2.   Handicapped children—Family
relationships—Addresses, essays, lectures.   I.   Brown,
Sara L., 1940–   II.   Moersch, Martha S.
LC4015.P28 1978   371.9   78–18517
ISBN 0–472–09302–9
ISBN 0–472–06302–2 pbk.

At the editors' request, their royalties will be paid to the Institute for the Study of Mental Retardation and Related Disabilities.

Portraits by Jeanne deYoung Bright

Early Intervention Project—Outreach
Institute for the Study of Mental Retardation and Related Disabilities
The University of Michigan

*To all the parents
who have taught us*

Preface

Early in 1973, a pilot program was started at the Institute for the Study of Mental Retardation and Related Disabilities for children from birth through four years of age with any type of handicapping condition. Each week a home visit was made and the children attended one group session. A major focus of both home and group sessions was to help parents assume major roles in the management and treatment of their children. Parents were active participants in all areas of programming.

Federal funding from the "First Chance" network of the Handicapped Children's Early Education Program, Bureau of Education for the Handicapped, United States Office of Education, began in October 1973 for the Early Intervention Project for Handicapped Infants and Young Children. One of the major objectives of this project was to support parents as primary treatment providers for their handicapped children.

After two public school systems assumed continuation of the project service model in June 1976, Early Intervention Project-Outreach was also funded by the "First Chance" network. The purpose of this second project is to provide consultation and in-service training to school systems and other agencies wishing to develop early intervention programs. Through the assistance of project staff members, various school systems and other agencies have replicated the project's model. Assistance in working with parents has been a frequent request from these agencies, and project staff members have presented many workshops, seminars, and conferences on the various facets of parent involvement. Parents of project children have taken active roles in these training sessions.

As parent involvement was practiced in the direct service component or discussed in the training sessions, it became evident that we were working toward much more than teaching parents specific therapeutic exercises or how to stimulate language in young children. We were hoping that parents would acquire the confidence and skills needed to become advocates for their handicapped children in all areas of life—not only in relation to education, but also in areas of health, legal rights, religion, family and community life, and human fulfillment.

In view of these needs, this publication has three purposes: one, to assist other programs for young handicapped children in actively involving parents; two, to point out to professionals and parents the various advocacy roles parents can play in securing services for their handicapped children; and three, to remind all persons working with parents of handicapped children that the parenting of these children is a twenty-four-hour-a-day job which reaches far beyond the school grounds.

While experience gained in the two projects provided the rich background from which much of the material is drawn, the information has been generalized to illustrate what might take place in any early intervention program.

SARA L. BROWN
MARTHA S. MOERSCH

Explanatory Note: The terms *disabled, special,* and *handicapped* are generic terms used by various writers. In this volume, they are used interchangeably throughout the book to describe a person who:

1. has a disability which is attributable to a physical or mental impairment, such as cerebral palsy, mental retardation, autism, brain damage, blindness, deafness, loss of limb, or seizure activity causing ongoing concern; and
2. has involvement serious enough to require therapy and care in one or more of the developmental areas (language, social, cognition, self-care, fine/perceptual motor or gross motor); and
3. is performing significantly below normal in one of the developmental areas; and
4. manifests a handicapping condition from an early age; and
5. has a chronic disability which persists despite treatment or medication.

Contents

MARTHA S. MOERSCH

History and Rationale for Parent Involvement

The first years of the seventies may be known as the period in which concern for parental involvement in all aspects of child rearing and training reached its height. Newspapers and household magazines are as likely to contain articles on parenting as are professional journals and books. These publications range from explaining the rights of parents to describing methods of how parents can be more assertive and more influential; they have been directed to parents of normal children as well as parents of handicapped children. The role of parents as "teachers" has had much publicity, especially in the controversy over whether or not parents should teach their children to read as early as two or three years of age.

Writings directed to parents of normal children were influenced by the findings of Bruner (1970) and others that the early years were the years of most rapid growth; by the sputnik developments which spurred the need for increased technical knowledge; and by the recognition of the right of disadvantaged populations, whether of socioeconomic, cultural, or educational causes. More recently the rights of individuals to their own life styles have been promoted, even if the life styles had previously been considered deviant.

Recognition of the positive and negative results of specific child rearing practices over the world, research findings on the results of institutionalization, and interest in mother-child attachment have contributed to the trend toward increased emphasis on involvement of parents in all aspects of their children's lives.

All of these directions of change have benefited handicapped populations; some because of their universal application to all people, others because of the readiness of care-providers of handicapped populations to point out the special relevance of the changes to handicapped individuals and their families. Without the changes, it is unlikely that deinstitutionalization, mandatory special education laws, or laws outlawing discrimination of all types would have occurred.

It is always difficult to determine which sociological changes came first, and this has been true in the history of parent involvement in the care and education of their handicapped children. The organization of the Association for Retarded Children (now changed to Association for Retarded Citizens) and other parent organizations in the 1950s has greatly influenced provisions for handicapped children. Research findings of Skeels and Dye (1939) documented the advantages of family care for high-risk children. President Kennedy's family is credited with the resulting legislation which provided for the care of mentally retarded persons and for the training of personnel to provide the care.

Results of increased funding and programming showed families what could be accomplished and possibly led to the passage of state mandatory special education laws and to the federal Education of All Handicapped Children Act of 1975 (P.L. 94–142). The federal act and many of the state laws require that positive efforts be made to identify the population of handicapped children in order to provide services. Parents are seen as being in the best position to observe children and to identify children needing help.

Parental pressure encouraged legislators to recognize the rights of parents to seek benefits for their children and to pass laws which meet the needs of handicapped children. The proposed laws mandated programs for the children of parents seeking help and for children not yet identified as needing help. Legislation then provided programs, such as the various Child Find programs, to identify children who are candidates for special programs. Many Child Find projects have used newspapers, radio, television, publications, and public forums to educate parents in recognizing developmental delays in the growth and development of their children.

Along with the interplay of parents and those in positions to influence programming support, other potential program planners, including educators, psychologists, and health care professionals, have speculated on how the help could be provided, how parents could be involved in the programs, and how direct providers might be convinced to involve the parents. It has been necessary to consider both the cooperation and the methods to be used when parents and care providers decide to work together.

It was assumed in the past that parents provided care for their children twenty-four hours a day until they reached school age and for all of the day, except from eight to three, after the age of six. It was also assumed that parents and school personnel had the time, money, and knowledge to do what had to be done. Children not in the circumstances noted were placed in orphanages or other appropriate institutions; education was provided for those children able to take advantage of conventional educational programs. Sociological, moral, and legal constraints have changed the status of children, parents, and schools.

Various terms have been used to describe the relationship of handicapped children and their parents; it is assumed that this relationship includes the usual parent-child relationship plus the additional attention required by the handicapping condition. The term *parent involvement* does not necessarily carry an active connotation; however, persons advocating that parents should be involved in the care and education of their handicapped children assume active participation.

Several decades ago writers chose to use the term *management, counseling,* or *treatment* of parents, and parents played passive rather than active roles in programs for their children. There was much concern with fostering the *acceptance* of the handicapped child. In dealing with these concepts, the emphasis was often on trying to erase the neurotic tendencies of the parents (Wolfensberger and Kurtz, 1969). Education played a minor role in handicapped child care; custodial care was often the only solution, and custodial care was associated with medical and/or psychiatric management. Because of lack of knowledge as to what techniques were useful for the child, or the belief that nothing could change the condition of the child, developing parental acceptance was often considered to be part of the medical model, whether carried out by medical personnel or others.

In contrast, when it was recognized that even severely handicapped children could benefit from training, the educational model came into use. Ideally, the involvement model is active participation in both the medical model and the educational model through collaborative problem solving, mutual decision making, and practical management of day-to-day tasks of life.

Today's professional personnel, whether medical or educational, are prepared to recognize the feelings parents have upon learning that their child is handicapped. They look upon these feelings as natural, rather than neurotic. Denial of the problem is necessary at the beginning in order to allow the family to survive, but most parents "gradually accept the handicap and begin to learn how to deal with it" (Judge Baker Guidance Clinic, 1974). Olshansky (1969), urges the professional worker to "abandon the simplistic and static concept of parent acceptance," since all parents both accept and reject their children at different times. He goes on to ask, "How much progress would have been achieved in the field of rehabilitation if the issue of 'acceptance' had been made the primary focus of professional concern rather than the issue of managing the disability most efficiently through the use of prosthetic devices?" Instead of dwelling on the "chronic sorrow" of the parents, the professional person should accept the idea that chronic sorrow is a natural, rather than a neurotic, reaction.

Parents need the understanding of professionals, but they also need concrete services to help them in managing and living with the handicapped child. Some parents of older handicapped children have reported that they always had plenty of people to talk with them about their feelings of having a handicapped child, but it was very hard to find someone who could tell them what to do with feeding, toileting, or behavior problems.

Current literature contains references to the value of parent involvement in relation to the child, the parents, and the teacher. "Teacher," as used here, is a general term and applies to all who provide educationally related programming for handicapped children. The majority of publications relate to the teacher, and usually to the special education teacher. As younger and more handicapped children become the "students," the "teacher" may be an occupational or physical therapist or a nurse.

Value to the Child
Examples of the benefits of parent involvement to the child are noted as: (1) the teaching style used by the mother is very important in shaping early motivation and cognitive functioning (Lillie, 1975); (2) much early learning occurs in the child's home environment with the mother, or mother surrogate, as primary "teacher," even if the

child is enrolled in some type of day care center (Lillie, 1975); (3) the center's program may have little effect on the child if not planned in consistency with the home environment (Lillie, 1975); and (4) "Programs that train and motivate parents . . . are essential to ensure early and continuing care of the child" (Schaefer, 1974). Parent involvement has a practical aspect in that "a handicapped child has to work so much harder for everything he learns that it seems scarcely necessary to teach him two different approaches to such things as tying his shoes just because mother and teacher didn't get together" (Boggs, 1969).

In a review of the effectiveness of early intervention programs, Bronfenbrenner (1974) concludes that while the documentation and research designs are not usually as well developed as is desirable, to the extent that valid conclusions can be drawn at all, only those programs which have a strong component of parent involvement are effective.

Value to Parents
Some of the benefits of parent involvement to the parents are: (1) parents need to feel "adequate" (Cansler and Martin, undated), to feel "competent" (Lillie, 1975), to increase their ability to "cope" with the child's behavior and special problems (Nardine, 1974), and to feel that they are doing something "concrete" (Nardine, 1974); (2) parents can meet classroom objectives with non-classroom techniques and thus provide therapy for the special child on a twenty-four-hours-a-day, seven-days-a-week basis; although, unfortunately, the parents of the special child are a neglected therapeutic resource on the rehabilitation scene (Barsch, 1969); and (3) parent involvement provides a mutual support system for parents (Lillie, 1975).

Recognition of the value of parent involvement comes from many sources, including: (1) persons working in early childhood education who recognize the critical importance of working with parents. Parents need an even more central role in the development of handicapped children (Cohen, 1975); (2) special education literature confirms a "growing favor among professional educators toward constructive parental involvement" (Kelly, 1974, p. 18); (3) the "greater long-term effectiveness of parent-centered as contrasted to child-centered early education programs suggests that child health [and educational] programs should have a major goal of supporting family care of the child" (Schafer, 1974); (4) parent groups made up of parents of children not yet in school, children in school, and children beyond school age (Barsch, 1969); and (5) militant parent groups that have led to the recognition of the need for a national effort to deal with children with learning disorders. Because of the different needs of the learning disabled child, this national effort may stimulate development of a more intelligent involvement of parents in the educational process of all children (Barsch, 1969).

Value to Teachers
Teachers benefit in a variety of ways from parent involvement, including a new form of parental relationship in which the parent is in a direct, personal, and continuous partnership with the teacher, representing a significant opportunity to improve the efficiency of special education in every disability category (Barsch, 1969).

Much program growth in special education has been the result of constructive parental influence on public policy and legislation (Kelly, 1974). Parents are prime consumers of services in child development centers, and as consumers paying through fees or taxes, they should receive the type of services they want (Lillie, 1975). One of the basic facts of educational life of the 1970s is the revolt of the taxpayer and the demand for quality education. Millage votes for increased taxes for schools lose, not only because of their cost, but also because meaningful involvement has so long been discouraged (Kelly, 1974).

Federal legislation, which supports many state and local programs, requires that the programs involve parents. Such a prerequisite further ensures the working relationship between parents and teachers.

How Parents Can Best Be Involved
Bronfenbrenner (1971) believes that parents must be involved in the activities of the school and the home with emphasis on direct interaction with the child and on the strengthening of enduring emotional ties between the child and parents.

Northcott (1972), who has been involved in programs for young deaf children, cautions programs to be aware of the special situations of the single parent, the parent in a multigeneration family under one roof, and the very young parent resisting the "establishment."

Pannor (1973) states: "If we are to be effective and reach large numbers of people, we need to employ more approaches that add to a family's adequacy so that they can feel more secure and confident in doing their own problem-solving and continue to develop on their own."

Gold (1975) indicates that we must "develop parent involvement programs which increase the parents' skills and sense of competency and which help parents feel at ease in the school setting."

There are many references to the ways in which school programs can involve parents as volunteers, teacher aides, providers of special services such as construction of toys and other equipment, teaching associates, auxiliary teachers, participants at parent meetings and individual conferences, and in other ways. There is a small, but growing number of references to parents as treatment providers or as teachers.

The references also note that there are problems in involving parents in programs. Barsch (1969) notes that special education teachers are well trained in meeting the needs of the child, but poorly trained in meeting the needs of parents. He concludes that, generally, the parent is more favorably inclined toward the teacher than the teacher is toward the parent. Kelly (1974) says that many teachers feel that education, and especially special education, is now too complex and important a process to allow for much parent involvement, but he places essential responsibility for parental involvement with the teacher, calling it a professional responsibility of the teacher.

What Changes Will Parent Involvement Bring?
If parental involvement is a force to be reckoned with in the coming decade, how can it be placed in its proper perspective of practical application in the day-to-day educational process for children who have the special needs which make them eligible for special education programming? The question becomes even more germane when state after state lowers the age for public school responsibilities to birth. For those persons who feel that the numbers of handicapped children are too small, or who doubt that the outcomes of programs for handicapped children are impressive enough to justify the cost, the recurring comment on the need to provide early childhood education for all three- and four-year-old children may force even larger numbers of persons to wrestle with the issue of parental involvement in education programs for all young children. An increased general awareness may provide even more assistance for handicapped children.

If deinstitutionalization becomes more of a reality in all states, parents will have a closer and longer contact with their handicapped children than was true in the past. It is hoped that parent involvement started early in the infant's training program will prepare parents to be productively involved as the child's age increases. Even though no state but Michigan has mandatory special education laws providing programs to the age of twenty-five, many do include programs up to age twenty-one. As yet, the schools do not appear to be developing programs which will prepare students for work settings; sheltered workshops are few in number, and the economic and social climates do not promise sufficient numbers of service jobs which could be held by less severely handicapped adults.

Just as parents have lobbied for education and other services for school-aged children, it is hoped that they will be able to secure appropriate living and work facilities as their children reach adulthood. Hopefully, parent involvement can be sustained beyond the infant and school-aged levels to adolescence and adulthood in a manner that will encourage attainment of maximal independence on the part of handicapped persons.

There is a need for research studies to be done on: parent rating scales; methods of teaching parents to write objectives for their child; growth and development charts which are understandable to parents of low intellectual and/or educational levels; data which will assist teachers in working with parents of various cultural and socioeconomic levels; mother-child attachment studies; and information which leads to understanding the relationship of parents to siblings of the handicapped child, to extended family members, to neighbors, to friends, and to each other as husband and wife, as well as father and mother. There is an equal need for those who encourage parent involvement to keep in mind that suggestions for tasks which are time consuming must be kept within a realistic perspective of overall family needs.

REFERENCES

Barsch, R. L. 1969. *The Parent Teacher Partnership* (Arlington, Va.: Council for Exceptional Children).

Boggs, E. M. 1969. "Pointers for Parents," in *Management of the Family of the Mentally Retarded,* ed. E. W. Wolfensberger and R. A. Kurtz (Chicago: Follett), p. 500.

Bronfenbrenner, U. 1974. "Is Early Intervention Effective?" *Report on Longitudinal Evaluations of Preschool Programs,* vol. 2, no. (OHD) 76–30025 (Washington, D.C.: U.S. Department of Health, Education, and Welfare).

————. 1971. "Who Cares for America's Children?" *Young Children* 26, no. 3, pp. 157–63.

Bruner, J. S. 1970. "Infant Education As Viewed by a Psychologist," in *Education of the Infant and Young Child,* ed. V. H. Denenberg (N.Y.: Academic Press).

Cansler, D. P. and Martin, G. H. Undated. *Working with Families* (Chapel Hill, N.C.: Chapel Hill Training–Outreach Project).

Cohen, S. 1975. "Integrating Children with Handicaps into Early Childhood Education Programs," *Children Today* 4, no. 1, pp. 15–17.

Gold, B. 1975. "Policy Statement of the Los Angeles School District Outreach Project," *Cycles* 3, no. 1, p. 5.

Kelly, E. J. 1974. *Parent-Teacher Interaction: A Special Educational Perspective* (Seattle, Wash.: Special Child Publications).

Judge Baker Guidance Clinic. 1974. *Responding to Individual Needs in Head Start,* no. (OHD) 75–1075 (Washington, D.C.: U.S. Department of Health, Education, and Welfare), p. 11.

Lillie, D. L. 1975. "The Parent in Early Childhood Education," *Journal of Research and Development in Education* 8, no. 2, pp. 7–13.

Nardine, F. 1974. "Parents as a Teaching Resource," *Cycles* 2, no. 8, pp. 7–13.

Northcott, W. L. 1972. "Developing Parent Participation," in *Parent Programs in Child Development Centers,* ed. D. L. Lillie (Chapel Hill, N.C.: University of North Carolina).

Olshansky, S. 1969. "Chronic Sorrow: A Response to Having a Mentally Defective Child," in *Management of the Family of the Mentally Retarded,* ed. E. W. Wolfensberger and R. A. Kurtz (Chicago: Follett), p. 118.

Pannor, H. 1973. "The Family Approach to School Problems in an Agency Setting," in *Family Roots of School Learning and Behavior Disorders,* ed. R. Friedman (Springfield, Ill.: Charles C. Thomas), p. 193.

Schaefer, E. S. 1974. "A Perspective on Developmental Assessment under EPSDT," in *Health Care Screening and Developmental Assess-*

ment, ed. S. P. Hersch and S. Rojcewicz (Rockville, Md.: National Institute of Mental Health), p. 36.

Skeels, H. M. and Dye, H. B. 1939. "A Study of the Effects of Differential Stimulation on Mentally Retarded Children," *Proceedings and Addresses of the American Association on Mental Deficiency* 44: 114–36.

Wolfensberger, E. W. and Kurtz, R. A., eds. 1969. *Management of the Family of the Mentally Retarded* (Chicago: Follett).

Parents as Advocates

PAULA VUKOVICH

He's a Child First

Not all parents are given a complete diagnosis at the birth of their child. With our son, diagnosis has been an ongoing process which, although he is now five, is probably still not altogether complete.

After a very short but strenuous labor, my husband and I gave birth to a beautiful seven-pound, thirteen-ounce boy. We wanted this child so much and had brought this product of our love into the world with such joy and excitement—how could he be anything less than perfect? Our triumph was crushed with the knowledge that our son, whom we already loved dearly, had been born without eyes. Doctors had also detected a heart murmur which they promised to follow closely. I looked at my husband, who was at that point as white as a sheet, took his hand, and said, "We'll make it." It wasn't until the following morning that I felt the full impact of what had happened to us. Bill had been through his crisis and was ready to give me the support I needed. Telling his parents, who lived so far away, that they finally had their grandson but that he wasn't perfect, was one of the hardest tasks I have ever had to undertake. I felt that I had failed everyone I loved. It was at that point that my days, months, and years of coping began.

Our son came home with us only two days after his birth. He was delightful, so happy and content. He fed at my breast eagerly. Our child was blind. We accepted that and we were prepared to give him everything he needed. After all, there are lots of happy and very capable blind people in the world.

13

We were to have several experiences with the medical world. The next was at a nearby hospital clinic where David, at two weeks of age, was given a sonar test to determine if he had an optic nerve. He did not and was labeled "anophthalmic." We were sent to ophthalmology where we were abruptly told that he must be fitted with prosthetic eyes as soon as possible. Our feelings weren't even considered, and at that point we just had too much to cope with so we refused.

Our next contact was David's pediatrician, who has been one of my major sources of support through the past five years. By the time our son had reached his third month, it was time for a cardiac evaluation. He tolerated the long, tedious day of X rays, an electrocardiogram, and physical examinations as well as could be expected. Finally, by late afternoon, the head of cardiology came into the little room where we had been waiting and told us that David had "tetralogy of Fallot." He advised us to postpone surgery until David grew larger and more demands could be placed on his heart. We returned to the clinic every six months thereafter and received the same diagnosis.

By the age of three, our son had developed some very real behavior problems. Even though we loved him very much, there were days when he was almost impossible to tolerate. He slept only two or three hours at night and didn't take daytime naps. Pain of severe constipation caused him to cry for hours. His doctors felt it was due to poor circulation related to his heart problem. David developed self-abusive behaviors, such as punching his head, poking his chin, and biting his hand to the point of drawing blood.

Our son just wasn't developing the way he should. He wasn't sitting, wasn't interested in exploring, and resisted physical manipulation. Not only was he delayed, but he was irritable and difficult to handle. A pediatric psychiatrist had told us that anophthalmic children develop more slowly than other blind children, but we decided to seek out a neurologist to ease our minds. A physical examination and an electroencephalogram revealed very definite brain damage. Our suspicions became reality. Our son was not only blind but mentally retarded, an even more severe condition. The neurologist could give us no guarantee that our son would even master the most basic skill of walking. We discussed David's severe sleeping problem and a mild bedtime sedative was recommended. I resisted initially but was so overwhelmed with constant exhaustion that I could barely function, let alone be a good mother. Our son's pediatrician made me realize that if a sedative could make David feel more rested, it would probably improve his functioning and was worth a try. The results were immediate. David began to sleep for longer periods at night and his disposition was much improved. Life was much more pleasant.

A month before his fourth birthday, David was due for another evaluation at the cardiac clinic. I was not prepared for the appalling recommendations given to me that day. The doctor I had once trusted and respected was now telling me that our son was not worth his investment. He was refusing David's needed surgery on the basis of his retardation. I was too deeply hurt to fight and feebly suggested that surely surgery would help my son if it would increase his oxygen supply. It was quite obvious to me that David would feel better and want to do more. But I was dealing with a man who had made his decision, and I was getting nowhere. Blinded by tears of hurt and fury, I scooped up a very tired, cranky little boy and somehow managed to drive home, where I told my story to Bill. By the next day my hurt had turned to anger. I called our son's pediatrician and demanded an appointment that evening. He was very sympathetic. This was not a new story to him at all, and he recommended another cardiologist in a nearby city. After my anger had subsided, I thought that perhaps our son's heart defect did not need immediate attention. It was a year before I called the new cardiologist.

Little did we know what this new hospital clinic had in store for our five-year-old son when we arrived for yet another evaluation. The tests were completed, and we were given the results in a little more than an hour. The cardiologist strongly recommended a catheterization. Fully anticipating to return home with our son, we were told that David's heart condition was serious; immediate surgery was advised. These doctors were anxious to help him. To them he was a child first. His handicaps were only part of the total person who, in their opinion, had just as much right to good health as a normal child born with everything intact. This operation was fairly successful, but David will need further surgery in the future. On David's discharge day, we were told the results of tests done during his hospitalization. The geneticist had arrived at the conclusion that David's defects were probably caused by prenatal exposure to several viruses. They also discovered that he has a hypothyroid condition. We were told to return in a month for further tests and treatment. Ophthalmology was consulted and again, the question of prosthetic eyes was raised. We had decided against them because we want people to accept David for what he is. The prostheses would be purely cosmetic and would not affect his functioning. David would also have to undergo surgery of his eye sockets, at quite an expense.

Our little fellow had been through a long, hard month, but his recovery was remarkable; he returned to school, a program for the severely mentally impaired, a month later. By Christmas, two months after surgery, David began to show signs of improvement. His disposition had improved remarkably, and he obviously felt much better. Now he is actually happy most of the time and more of a delight to live with.

Recently our son's physical therapist became concerned about David's hips. Upon further examination by his pediatrician, I was advised to take David to an orthopedist. He found a slight dislocation, especially on the right side. Once again we were met with another challenge.

Coping with our son's disability has certainly been an ongoing process, and we hope and pray that we finally have a total picture of our severely impaired little boy. As a result, I feel I've grown from a child myself to a mature adult capable of handling the problems and frustrations involved in raising a multiply handicapped child. Only when we have exhausted all possibilities and taken advantage of every opportunity can the guilt we feel be eased. Then the ever present question "Have I done enough for my child?" can be answered. We parents don't have to be at the mercy of the medical profession. We have the right to make our own decisions, seek a second opinion if we are dissatisfied, and fight if we feel our child is being shortchanged. This beautiful little child, with all his imperfections, has opened up a whole new world for me: new responsibilities, new challenges, and a hope that someday our "forgotten children" will fit into a society which still remains somewhat hostile.

VIRGINIA S. NELSON

The Pediatrician's Role

Pediatricians are trained to care for the health and illnesses of children, but only rarely is working with parents, especially parents of handicapped children, included in their curriculum. As medical students, they study normal structure and function of the human body, then abnormal structure and function. They learn about genetics and about pharmacology; how to make diagnoses by taking medical histories, administering physical examinations, and studying laboratory and radiologic results.

During their postgraduate training, interns and residents refine these medical skills and become responsible for the care of patients. Interviewing techniques may be included during this training, but learning to work with parents usually comes from two sources only: from one's own skills and experience and/or from observing one's teachers. How good these teacher-models are depends upon the circumstances of the training; how well one learns from these models depends upon oneself.

The system for training pediatricians presented above may sound haphazard and likely to produce poorly trained clinicians. In fact, pediatricians trained in American training programs are, for the most part, well trained. They do have good models in their preceptors and they do become good clinicians. Training leading to certification in pediatrics, however, does not require the physician to develop skills in working with parents. The problem of having just any pediatrician work with parents and their handicapped child is one which families of handicapped children encounter when they seek a pediatrician.

Assuming that a pediatrician is trained to work well with parents, his role is vital in encouraging parent involvement. From the time a diagnosis of a problem is made or suspected, the physician can help parents work through their feelings to become active participants in the medical care of their child.

Klaus and Kennell in their book *Maternal-Infant Bonding* (1976) have an excellent discussion on working with parents of a newborn with a congenital malformation. Much of their discussion can be extended to include working with parents of a child newly diagnosed as being handicapped. They first discuss the five stages of emotional reactions parents go through upon learning of their child's problem:

> First stage: shock
> Second stage: disbelief (denial), "It's not really true."
> Third stage: sadness, anger, anxiety; the anger may be directed at the child, at a professional, at someone else, or at self
> Fourth stage: equilibrium—a lessening of intense emotional reactions
> Fifth stage: reorganization

All parents go through these stages, but at varying rates and with varying intensities.

The physician's initial role in parent involvement should be at the time a diagnosis is first made or suspected. He can help parents go through these stages by providing counseling and serving as a model of acceptance of the handicapped child. Klaus and Kennell also provide good recommendations for care:

1. Bring the baby to the mother as soon as possible. Images of an abnormal infant are usually worse than reality. (This assumes diagnosis is made in a newborn.)
2. Emphasize the normality of the child.
3. Avoid tranquilizers for the parents.
4. Explain findings.
5. Show acceptance of the child.
6. Encourage communication between the parents.
7. Encourage the parents to explain the situation to friends and relatives.

Once parents have passed through the first two stages of emotional reaction (and even before, for some parents), the physician must enlist the parents' help in caring for their child. First comes learning about the child's special needs. This will progress in steps for most parents, since most of us plan only for the immediate future. Physicians must clearly explain the child's needs, emphasizing the normality as much as possible; they must also provide as much information as possible about the problem. Written material is especially helpful for some parents.

The physician must help parents learn that their own attitudes and those they instill in their child may be the most important factors in determining how well their child adjusts. The following two case histories may serve as illustrations.

Carla is a seven-year-old child who is severely handicapped with spina bifida. Looking at a list of her many problems, one would imagine she would be confined to bed and totally dependent. Her parents, however, have always expected her to be as independent as possible and have instilled this attitude in her. As a result, she is now in a regular, second grade class, even though she is confined to a wheelchair and must have help in some of her activities of daily living.

Tommy is now eleven and he, too, has spina bifida. His problems are mild, compared to Carla's, but his family has always babied him and emphasized his handicap to him. Now he is dependent on his family in most areas, even though he has the physical potential to be nearly independent.

The differences between Tommy and Carla are the result of many factors. Perhaps if the professionals working with Tommy's family had helped them accept his normality and helped them guide him toward independence, the outcome would have been different.

In summary, the pediatrician's role in parent involvement starts with his training, when he seeks out models of physicians who work well with parents (especially parents of handicapped children) and learns from them.

Once a physician suspects or diagnoses a problem, he must then work with the child's parents by:

1. clearly explaining the problem to the parents;
2. helping the parents work through their feelings about having a child with a problem; these feelings usually include shock, denial, sadness, anger, anxiety, equilibrium, and reorganization;

3. emphasizing the child's normality;
4. accepting the child and helping the parents to accept the child;
5. helping parents learn about their child's special needs;
6. helping parents learn how their own attitudes will affect their child; and by
7. helping parents motivate their child to accomplish to the limits of his ability.

A physician who works with parents in these areas is a valuable member of the intervention team.

REFERENCES

Klaus, M. and Kennell, J. 1976. *Maternal-Infant Bonding* (St. Louis: C.V. Mosby).

Lindemann, E. 1944. "Symptomatology and Management of Acute Grief," *American Journal of Psychiatry* 101:141–48.

ELEANOR W. LYNCH

The Home-School Partnership

The Nature of the Partnership

Until recently, parent involvement meant baking cookies for the Halloween party, driving a station wagon load of kids to the zoo, or serving faithfully as the PTA president or membership chairman. Teachers and administrators were grateful for the help, and those parents who worked tirelessly in these efforts were rewarded with lapel pins and praise. The lines were carefully drawn; parents were welcome to *help* but not allowed to *participate* in the day-to-day workings of the organization which would occupy approximately 14,040 hours of their child's time during his most important years of physical and psychological growth.

In the late sixties, things began to change. The watershed years for so many other sociopolitical changes, the sixties also heralded a change in educational practices. Initially, through the writings of Kozol, Rosenthal, Silberman, and others, the biases of the educational institution were exposed, and those who read and heard were outraged. A few advantaged parents started their own schools; free schools and alternative schools sprang up; cooperative preschools flourished; and the federal government established Head Start, the first national educational effort that mandated a role for parents in their child's education. But, as always, some people missed the revolution. Public school classrooms remained essentially unchanged.

As with other innovations in education, the recent efforts to invest parents with power in educational decision making have come out of special education. And, as with many other inno-

21

vations, it came not from rigorous research or a long process of professional self-examination and growth, but from a piece of federally mandated folk wisdom. The thinking went something like this: children with handicaps need extra educational help; the sooner we provide the help, the better the chance they will have to develop maximally; how early can we begin? why not with infants?; but, you can't send babies to school; you can if their parents go, too. Voilà, parent involvement!

So, from a rather inauspicious beginning of heightened consciousness in the sixties, to the early intervention programs and the state and federal laws guaranteeing all handicapped children an education, parent involvement has become the keystone of many programs that followed. Education, at least for members of our society with handicaps, has become a partnership.

Becoming A Partner
Partnership implies an equality in the relationship between home and school, parents and teachers. In a business with such high stakes as helping children with handicaps to develop maximally, there can be no junior partners. For all of us, educators and parents alike, these roles are new. They require new ways of thinking, relating, and growing; like new shoes, they may hurt a bit.

So, how does one become a partner, a member of a team that is committed to working toward the good of a youngster with special needs? Here are some guidelines.

1. As a parent or educator, keep the child's needs uppermost in your mind. As an administrator, don't get trapped into serving the system and maintaining the status quo. Think about the child first and your boss second. As a parent, don't get trapped into looking for a program just to make your life easier or because that's what the Jones boy gets. Try to decide what your child needs to learn next, how he learns best, and look for a program that provides it.

2. As an educator, don't be afraid to admit you don't know. Few educators have been formally trained to work with handicapped infants and young children. Fewer still have been trained to consult with parents. It is difficult to move from the position of an unchallenged authority to the learner, but it is the most important step. Knowing all the answers is not only impossible, it's bad modeling. Parents'

self-confidence can grow immeasurably when they see that even the experts need help. Even for experts, there is no package of skills and knowledge that will fix everything.

3. As a parent, don't be afraid to tell the educators what you *do* know about your child. Educators have the advantage of having worked with many children, but you have the advantage of knowing your child better than anyone else in the world. You know his likes and dislikes, style of learning, fears, joys, strengths, and weaknesses. Share that invaluable information.

4. As an educator, remember that parental priorities may be different from yours. Although you may see toilet training as the number one objective in the child's program, the parents may not. Make compromises on these issues a habit.

5. As a parent, check your family priorities for the child against those of the larger community; ignoring objectives that are important in your community may further handicap your child.

6. As a parent or educator, don't ignore adults' needs for a pat on the back now and then. It's nice to know that when the teacher calls, it might be because Matt has had a good day; or when a parent calls, it might be something other than a complaint about the bus schedule. Parenting and teaching handicapped children are hard work. All of us need to hear that someone else thinks we're doing a good job.

7. As a parent, don't forget that the educator is usually working with fifteen to twenty other children and families who want his undivided attention. As an educator, don't forget that the handicapped child is not the only member of the family. The husband, wife, brothers, sisters, grandparents, aunts, and cousins all have needs and make demands.

8. As a parent or educator, remember that you are both working toward the same goal—the maximal development of the handicapped child. If either of you is beginning to feel frustrated, hurt, left out, disappointed, threatened, afraid, or angry, talk to each other. Discover what's going wrong, and work together to change it.

Maintaining the Partnership
One of the disappointments of adulthood is discovering that

maintaining good relationships is often more difficult than making them. The same is true within the home-school partnership. It is often much easier for the parent and educator to work together with an infant, than with an eight-year-old or eighteen-year-old. Enthusiasm runs high with young children, even when they are handicapped. It is too early to see limits; there is always the chance that our efforts will be rewarded with some miraculous change. As the child gets older, the limits become clearer, the labels more easily said, and enthusiasm wanes.

At this point, even the professional may have difficulty facing the reality that all of the training, skill, and caring isn't really going to produce dramatic changes. Parents, as well, are reaching another phase in acceptance of their child as reality forces its way through hope. When both partners are in pain in any relationship, it is easy to be distrusting, blaming, cynical, and closed. This is no less true in the home-school partnership than in any other relationship. It is often during this time that parents threaten to sue the school and educators give up on working with "that unrealistic family." Sometimes families are unrealistic, and sometimes lawsuits are the only way to right wrongs, but a reexamination of the basis for our feelings should come first. This is the time to open communication between parents, between home and school, and between all of the others who are pushing and pulling. This is the time to review the guidelines discussed above and to try them once again.

Advocacy

As parents and educators become more comfortable in a partnership, they will learn to be more effective. Though it may never be easy, it will become important enough to warrant the continual investment of self. The next logical step for the parent-educator team is one of advocacy. They can now move into the larger arena to work for the rights of other handicapped children and adults.

This pairing, of parent and educator, produces a powerful team. It can do more than either party can do alone—the primary reason for any partnership.

SALLY and RON JAWOROWSKI

A Baby Goes to "School"

When our daughter, Laura Ann, was born with Down's syndrome, we quite naturally wanted the best of everything for her; but we were unaware that an education would be available, or even possible, for her. As teachers, we both had years of experience in the traditional school setting and had some knowledge of general special education, but we knew nothing of special education programs for severely involved children, especially very young children. At that time, our state did not have a mandatory education law covering children from birth. We were fortunate, however, in that local mental health agencies had developed programs for handicapped infants.

Parents of all handicapped children share a similar hope: they want the best education possible for their child. Many states have now passed laws to provide for the public education of handicapped children, offered at an earlier age than for other children. As soon as a mentally impaired child is born or diagnosed, parents need to begin learning about their state's laws regarding special education.

A telephone call to the local public school administration office is a good way to begin. You can quickly and easily find out at what age education begins for mentally impaired children. If your child is immediately eligible, tell them about his handicap and find out what procedures you need to follow to ensure immediate educational services. If your child is not currently eligible, find out what services he could utilize until he is eligible.

If your child meets the age requirement, the first step is usually a complete psychological evaluation of his development. We found

25

that this was the perfect place to begin taking an active role in being Laura's advocate. We asked permission to be present and observe the professionals' evaluations. We found that, in some cases, we could assist or perhaps suggest methods of eliciting our child's best performance, answer questions about her behavior and abilities at home, and determine for ourselves whether our child's responses were accurate portrayals of her abilities.

After the evaluation, there should be a joint meeting of all professionals and the parents; in Michigan, it's called an Educational Planning and Placement Committee (EPPC). In other states, it may be referred to as a parent informing or staffing meeting. At this time, the professionals present their evaluations of the child so that a placement can be made. After a placement has been determined, an Individual Educational Plan (IEP), in accordance with P.L. 94–142, is developed. Objectives are outlined and support staff members, such as a physical therapist and a speech therapist, are then assigned.

From the experience of other parents, we learned that we must be well prepared for these meetings. We found that this was one time when we needed someone to help plead Laura's cause—an advocate who could be more objective than we, who was familiar with these proceedings, and who was better able to understand the educational jargon used by the professionals. Our advocate was a staff member of the local Association for Retarded Citizens, but it could have been any professional or person who knew and/or had worked with Laura. Our advocate had us prepare questions that we wanted to ask; think of the specific goals and objectives, as well as long-range goals, we wanted to achieve; and had us consider what services we felt we needed, or might need. By encouraging us in our role as parents and helping us understand the program goals being outlined for Laura, our advocate provided support to us during the meeting.

When Laura was placed in her program, we wanted to meet all of the staff. We discovered that if we had at least met the staff, we would probably feel freer to contact them when we were serving as Laura's advocate in seeking help for her. The director, principal, or coordinator may not have much direct contact with each child, but he does have the responsibility for what happens in his school. If we let him know what we hope our child will learn or accomplish, he might be more likely to observe our child's progress on an informal basis.

The support staff—occupational therapist, physical therapist, speech therapist, social worker, and psychologist—have been valuable sources of help. The more they know about Laura and our personal goals, the better able they are to assist us in helping her reach these goals. In our experience, we have had tremendous cooperation from these professionals. Conferences are easily arranged, notes are written, and telephone calls are made so that we can keep in close contact with them. Recently we asked the physical therapist to evaluate Laura during a school therapy session, to determine whether she was ready to discontinue wearing high-top shoes. The physical therapist sent a note home with a full explanation, so we knew why Laura should continue wearing her present shoes. The therapist knows we are interested in Laura's physical development and continues to suggest activities for home therapy.

Laura's classroom teachers have the most direct contact with her, so we are continually in communication with them to express our feelings and concerns. A notebook is sent to and from school with her each day, in which we write notes to the teachers and they write them back to us. This is a marvelous and easy way to monitor Laura's daily progress. We have frequent telephone conferences, as well as more formal school conferences. Visits to the classroom are scheduled regularly. Since Laura is very limited in her ability to communicate, these methods of sharing ideas and concerns with the teachers are particularly valuable and helpful. Because of the open attitude of the teachers, we feel very free to serve as advocates in the classroom setting.

A coordinator from the school system makes regular home visits. Since she is responsible for coordinating all of the educational experiences for Laura, we make requests of her each time she comes to our home. For example, we have expressed a desire for more frequent swimming sessions in the school pool, different or new suggestions for activities to do at home to reach a specific goal, a list of books to read to provide us with background information on specific problems of our child, suggestions for community agencies that might help us, and an informal evaluation of progress being made. We have described activities that we have done at home that were helpful and others that we felt were not particularly successful. We have also asked her to be our advocate for Laura in certain instances at school.

The home visitors have not only taught us new skills, but have provided our sons with ideas for playtime activities with Laura. The visitors have been perceptive enough to include the boys when they wished to be included, but never to push them. Our sons have almost felt privileged to have a retarded sister because they have been included in the play and fun during Laura's home visits.

Psychological, speech, and other evaluations are periodically scheduled after a child is in a program. Although both of us cannot be present for the evaluations which occur during the school day, we feel that one of us should always be present when Laura is evaluated. During the last evaluation, one of us attended and was invited to participate, answer questions of the psychologist, and suggest methods for obtaining the best results from our child. Following the testing, a conference was set up for both of us and all the staff members working with Laura. At that conference we were able to discuss the evaluation results and what kinds of behavior we could expect to see next. Suggestions for home activities were made, and again we could express our personal goals for Laura. In this way, we were not building false hopes or developing unrealistic goals. A unified effort between school and home was again developed.

We have found it necessary to advocate for Laura with regard to the school bus. We needed to be sure that a seat appropriate to her size and type of handicap was provided for her. Since she was not sitting independently when she first began to ride the bus, we had to request an infant safety seat. As she has grown and developed, we've made sure that the appropriate safety changes have been made. As children grow and develop new behaviors, new seating arrangements need to be made. One of the older boys who sat in front of Laura on the bus was too large for his safety seat. He was able to turn and grab her and other children nearby. This was not only a dangerous seat for him, but it was frightening to her and the other young children. We were successful advocates; new seating arrangements were made to assure the safety and comfort of all the children.

Arrangements are needed if your child must take medication during the school day. The teacher, nurse, or secretary should be notified of this need and a mutually agreed upon schedule should be developed. Special eating problems or meal restrictions should be brought to the attention of the lunchroom staff. For instance, Laura has a tendency to gain weight and cannot tolerate gaseous foods. We've encouraged the staff to provide a diet in keeping with these needs.

School or classroom acceptance of a special child may be a problem that could be helped by the school librarian. She may be able to suggest books that deal with a similar problem. There are many books available that deal with a wide variety of handicaps. Some of our babysitters who have enjoyed caring for Laura have increased their interest and knowledge by reading books about the retarded. Some of the titles which we suggested were *David* (Roberts, 1968), *Don't Take Teddy* (Friis-Baastad, 1972), and *To Give an Edge* (Horrobin, 1975). Books have also been helpful to the siblings of a retarded child.

Communication and rapport with school professionals are the first steps toward effective parent advocacy. If you are already communicating with the staff, it is easier to take the next step—advocacy. You may be reluctant to advocate the first time, just as we were. We reminded ourselves, however, that it was for Laura's good, and that made it easier to do. As parents of a retarded child, we feel that advocating in school for our child is not just a privilege, but a responsibility that we are obligated to fulfill in order to ensure the best possible education for our daughter.

REFERENCES

Friis-Baastad, B. 1972. *Don't Take Teddy* (New York: Archway Paperback Books).
Horrobin, J. M. and Rynders, J. E. 1975. *To Give an Edge* (Minneapolis: The Colwell Press, Inc.).
Roberts, N. 1968. *David* (Richmond, Va: John Knox Press).

DIANE B. D'EUGENIO

But He Doesn't Fit in the Car Seat Anymore

How often have you been in the situation where your child can no longer use his car seat, or high chair, or baby bathtub because he has grown too large for it, but yet still requires its support because he has not yet developed the necessary skills to do without it? For parents of a handicapped child, this is a common situation. Its difficulty is compounded by the facts that suitable equipment often cannot be found in local stores and that you may not know how to find companies which make special equipment for handicapped children.

The purpose of this article is to provide you with information on equipment which is available to help you and your child carry out the daily living tasks of eating, toileting, bathing, dressing, and transporting. Whenever possible, commercially available products and equipment (and their adaptations) will be discussed, as well as equipment available from special supply companies. (See page 48 for further listings.)

On Buying Special Equipment

Before buying any piece of special equipment, you should give careful thought to what you are buying and what purpose the equipment will serve. The following considerations may be of help:

1. *Will the equipment meet your child's needs?*
   In considering this, you should first define what the prob-

lem is and the factors contributing to it, and then decide if the equipment will resolve the problem. For example, if the problem is that Johnny cannot feed himself, maybe it is because he cannot sustain his hold on the spoon. A spoon with a special handle might solve the problem. However, if Johnny cannot feed himself because he cannot raise the spoon to his mouth, then a special spoon will not solve the problem. After clarifying the problem and its contributing factors, search for equipment that is designed to meet the specific problem. Inquire whether you can have a trial period with the equipment to be certain it will be of help.

2. *How long will the equipment be needed?*
   Can the equipment be adjusted and made larger as your child grows? Will the equipment hold your child now and still be secure as he increases in weight? Is the material durable, washable, and fire resistant? What is the service and maintenance guarantee on the equipment? Is the equipment something your child will use for a short period of time, or for many years? Can the equipment be adapted to meet your child's changing developmental needs?

3. *What are the difficulties with the equipment?*
   The value of a piece of equipment will depend upon how well it fits your family's needs. Can you easily find space for larger equipment items in an appropriate room in your house? Will special chairs fit through necessary doorways? How transportable is the equipment? Can one person manage it? Does it allow your child to use the skills he has or does it make things so easy for him that he may lose the skills he already has?

4. *Can you afford to buy it?*
   For most families this is the first consideration. Before purchasing equipment, find out if you can borrow it from a hospital therapy department or from a school program. You may also be able to rent equipment from a pharmacy or household rental agency. If you decide to buy the equipment, the cost may be covered by your insurance policy; organizations such as Crippled Children's Services; local Easter Seal, March of Dimes, or cerebral palsy associations; or through community service clubs such as the Lions, Rotary, or Kiwanis.

5. *How do you find out about special equipment?*
   When seeking out special equipment, a good resource for you will be professionals involved in treating handicapped children. They usually have access to equipment catalogues, can advise you in making selections, and have information on financial help. They may also have ideas for modifying regular equipment or making special equipment from household items. Professionals to contact include occupational therapists, physical therapists, speech therapists, special education teachers, and physicians who are involved in pediatric rehabilitation.

While it is sometimes necessary to use special equipment with your child, remember that your ultimate goal is enabling your child to function without it; or, in cases of a severely handicapped child, to function with as little equipment as possible. It is important to realize that while the equipment may make it easier for your child to do the motor part of a task, you, not the equipment, will teach your child how to do the task.

In all areas of self-care and handling, it is important to encourage your child's maximum independent functioning. If your child is grabbing at the spoon during feeding, let him hold onto it as you feed him. If your child can hold his head upright, carry him so his head is not supported. If your child can pull his shirt off over his head, let him do it each time you undress him. You can also guide his hands to teach him other steps in taking off his shirt. Remember, all children will quickly learn to resist doing something they can do if mom and dad will do it for them.

Positioning
Proper positioning of your child is basic to the successful accomplishment of any task. Your child's sitting position should be symmetrical, which means that his weight is evenly distributed on both hips, his shoulders are forward with his arms in front of him, and his feet are flat on the floor or on a footrest. External support should be given only if your child needs it and then only to those parts of his body he cannot control. For a child with poor sitting balance, tie a strip of cotton webbing, a cloth diaper, or an old neck tie around his hips to support him and keep his hips at the correct angle. For a child with no trunk control, harness supports will provide the necessary external support. They are commercially

available (Baby Harness by Ambassador), available through a special equipment company (The Body Harness by Adaptive Therapeutic Systems), or can be homemade (fig. 1).

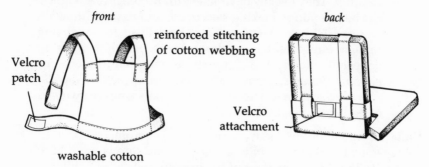

front   *back*

Velcro patch

reinforced stitching of cotton webbing

Velcro attachment

washable cotton

Fig. 1.   Body harness

Recommendations on best positions for your child will come from your child's therapist or teacher. Whatever positions are recommended, it is important that your child not spend all of his day in only one position and that the position not give him too much support since this could encourage inactivity.

Various chairs are available on the commercial market. The Cosco Go Seat (fig. 2) is a convertible three-inch- or six-inch-high child's chair with a back and low sides. It has two spaces in the back through which straps for a tie or harness can be inserted, or through which a strap can be inserted to secure it to a regular-size chair, thereby making it an inset chair. Cosco makes a second style of chair called Bottoms-Up Reversible Booster Seat (fig. 3). The height

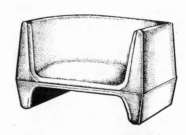

Fig. 2.   Cosco Go Seat   **Fig. 3.   Booster seat**

of this seat can be adjusted to either a three-inch or six-inch height by simply turning it over. It provides a nice sense of definable space for a blind child. To use it safely, a child would need moderate sitting balance, since it does not have a space for straps. Infant seats and high chairs will be discussed in the feeding section.

A child-size bean bag chair is good for children with very little sitting balance. It can be molded into various shapes, depending upon how much support your child needs. It also has more versatility for positioning than most chairs, since a child can be positioned on it lying on his back, his stomach, or side, as well as positioned in sitting. A possible drawback of the bean bag chair is that it might provide too much support, thereby encouraging inactivity.

Sturdy cardboard boxes can be made into a variety of chairs and tables. One style of chair which can be made is a modification of a corner chair. Select a cardboard box which is suitable to the child's size (comes to the height of the child's shoulders when sitting), cut the top off, and cut slots in the lower quarter of the sides (fig. 4). The front of the box can either be cut down or cut out and the box sides lined with foam, shelf liner, or a towel to reduce the rough edge of the box top. The box is then placed against the walls in the corner of a room for stabilization; insert straps, or an old neck tie, through the slots to secure the child in a sitting position. This seat can be used with children who can hold their head up well when sitting on your lap, but who do not have enough trunk control to sit alone on the floor.

A sturdy cardboard box can be inverted and made into a low table. Cut out a space in the front of the box for the chair (fig. 5).

Plastic or rubber foam is very useful material for adapting regular chairs and for cutting out new shapes for positioning a child.

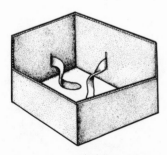

Fig. 4. Cardboard chair

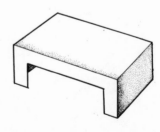

Fig. 5. Cardboard table

A square piece of thick (ten-inch) foam can be cut (fig. 6) and covered with fabric. By sitting the child in the semicircle cut-out, more trunk support can be provided. To be most effective, the foam should come to the height of the child's shoulders. For larger children, it may be necessary to stack two cutout shapes and cover them together to form one tall shape. Various other shapes of foam apparatus are available in special catalogues.

Bolsters are cylindrically shaped pieces of equipment used to position a child when lying on his stomach. A bolster can be made by simply rolling newspapers into a log, securing them with tape, and covering them with a towel; or it can be made by rolling towels into a log shape and securing them with wide masking tape. If a child has a tendency to roll off the bolster, it may be useful to insert a belt through the center of the roll and fasten it around the child (fig. 7).

Apparatus which can be used to position your child and which allows mobility includes scooter boards and sit-on moving toys. Scooter boards are commercially available (Crawl-a-gator) or can be made at home. Attach castors to a board which is cut to suit your child's height and cover it with foam or a piece of carpet. A variety of moving toys is available on the market, such as Tyke-Bike, Good Humor Bike, and the Fischer-Price Riding Horse. However, before making a choice, be certain it will be secure for your child to sit on safely.

Feeding

Positioning is especially important for feeding; proper positioning will make sucking, chewing, and swallowing easier for your child. It will also make self-feeding easier. The rule of symmetry should be

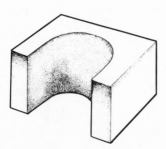

Fig. 6.   Foam chair

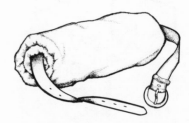

Fig. 7.   Towel bolster

followed whether your child feeds on your lap, in an infant seat, in a highchair, or at a regular table. This can be accomplished in the following ways.

Lap Feeding.   Hold your child so *both* his arms are brought forward by supporting him in the crook of your elbow and bringing his shoulders forward. Your chest will support him on one side and your forearm on the other. His hips will bend as you adjust him to an upright position (fig. 8).

Fig. 8.   Lap feeding

Infant Seat Feeding.   An infant seat allows you to have face-to-face contact with your child. This will encourage him to keep his head in midline, rather than turning it to the side. It frees your hands to feed him while maintaining his symmetrical position. Some infant seats offer various adjustments for upright and declining angles (Cosco Infant Seat and Dyn-o-mite Baby Car Seat and Carrier). However, all infant seats are generally small and therefore quickly outgrown.

High Chair Feeding.   High chairs and feeding tables which have tray space along the sides, as well as in front, offer more support for a child with poor sitting balance. They also provide useful space for a blind child to "search" for food or toys, in addition to giving him a sense of security. Adjustable seat backs and legs are useful features on a high chair or feeding table. Adjustable legs on a feeding table are particularly useful for maintaining the child's feet flat on a surface when he outgrows the footrest. A low bench or stool can also be used to support his feet. Adaptations for high chairs which encourage symmetrical sitting include a foam inset for the seat which will reduce the sitting area of the chair, thereby bringing the child's shoulders and trunk forward (fig. 9); rolled towels or diapers to make the seat space smaller; use of a tie or harness to give the

Fig. 9.   High chair foam inset

child trunk stability; Velcro straps around the footrest and over the child's feet to keep his feet flat on a surface; a horizontal bar on the tray for the child to hold on to for stabilization (especially needed for athetoid cerebral palsied children) and for maintaining shoulders and arms in forward positions (fig. 10).

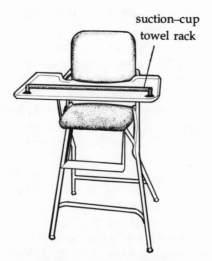

Fig. 10.   High chair stabilization bar

Table Feeding. The adaptations mentioned for high chairs also apply to table sitting. In order to encourage symmetrical sitting at a table, place an inset seat on a regular chair. A telephone book or large catalog under the base will raise the child's sitting height to the level of the table. Two types of child-size chairs which can be used as inset seats are Cosco's Go Seat and Bottoms Up Reversible Booster Seat. A high chair with the tray removed, or a bar seat which has armrests and a back, can also be used. A child's table and chair set has the advantage of appropriate size and height, allowing for symmetrical sitting, but the disadvantage of separating you from your child during a meal.

Equipment for Feeding. Many handicapped babies can use regular nipples or "premie" nipples. For the baby with a weak suck, the size of the nipple hole can be increased until the strength of the suck is better. If a child is able to hold his bottle but has not yet developed enough balance in sitting, or if the child is afraid to tip his head back as with some blind children, then bottles with a straw descending from the nipple can be used. Bottles in the shape of various animals (made by Gerber and Evenflo) provide especially nice tactile input for a blind child. Also commercially available are special medicine feeders. These consist of a nipple attached to a very tiny bottle with marked measures (Tommee Tippee Company).

Cup Feeding. A variety of children's drinking cups is available in stores. They come with one handle, two handles, or no handles; a weighted base or a regular base; with a top and a short spout, a top with a long spout, or with no top at all. The most suitable cup will depend on your child's needs. Generally, the specific features of these cups serve the following purposes: weighted-base cups prevent the cup from tipping over, even when put down unevenly; cups with spouts serve as the intermediate step in weaning a child from a bottle to a cup; cups with two handles allow the child to grasp and hold onto the cup more easily, by using two hands (this also ensures a good symmetrical position). Many parents have found paper cups to be best for teaching cup drinking, or the bathroom cup which usually has a rim for easier positioning of the lips. Many plastic cups can be cut to allow for "nose space" so a child can drink without having to tilt his head back.

Use of Utensils and Dishes. Many variations of spoons, forks, and knives are available through special equipment catalogs. For some of the commercial variations and suggestions for how they can be improvised from household materials see page 48.

Other special utensils which are available include a combination spoon and fork (Spork) and knives designed for people with use of only one hand.

One of the difficulties handicapped children have with dishes is that they move and slide on the table. This problem can be alleviated by using a dish with a suction-cup bottom and a rim around the edge. Such a combination is available on the commercial market (Tommee Tippee's Hot Plate Diner). Nonslip bowls can be made at home, by placing the dish on a rubber mat, such as a rubber gripper used to open jars, a thin piece of foam, or a Dycem mat (available in special equipment catalogs), or with double suction cups. Plate guards are available through special equipment catalogs or they can be improvised by bending a strip of aluminum and attaching it to the plate.

Use of Bibs.   Bibs made of various materials and with special "catch pockets" are available on the commercial market and come in large enough sizes to be used with three- and four-year-old children. Bibs can be made at home from old towels, diapers, tablecloths, or oilcloths, and a catch-all pocket can be easily added. To fasten the bib, Velcro (available in most fabric stores) can be used instead of ties or snaps. A bib/tablecloth made of plastic or washable fabric large enough to cover the feeding area can also be used. The easy clean-up feature of this bib may encourage the parent to allow the child to feed himself.

Toileting

The same considerations given to positioning for feeding should be applied to toileting. The best seat is one which offers a child the sitting support he needs, is low enough to allow his feet to touch the floor, and permits his trunk to lean slightly forward. A separate potty device is necessary for children with poor sitting balance or children afraid to sit on a potty seat when it is placed on a regular toilet. A potty chair offers security and support and can be used independently by a child, since he will not need the parent to lift him onto the toilet.

If you decide to purchase a potty chair, look for one which offers the amount of trunk support your child needs (a hip tie or harness support can also be used on a potty chair). Many available chairs come with a solid back, solid sides, or sides of wood slats and a tray in front. The height of most potty chairs is six inches, which is a good height for keeping the child's feet in contact with the floor. Several companies (Century, Cosco, Peterson) make potty chairs which look like miniature toilets. A child's back is supported when the seat cover is lifted. This type of potty chair has the advantage of looking like a regular toilet, which may make it easier for a severely retarded child to switch to a regular toilet when he outgrows the small one. A potty chair which doesn't have a tray or rail in front can still be used; simply position the child so he can hold onto the back of a child's size chair or a low towel rack placed in the bathroom.

Bathing

More commercial products designed to make bathing a baby safer and less of a strain on an adult's back have appeared on the market recently. These include child-size bathtubs and bathseats. The bathtubs come in two styles. One is an oblong inflated tube with a single layer of plastic in the center where the baby lies (Rub-a-Dub: Baby's First Bathtub by Young Royalty, Inc.). The center holds a small amount of water, thereby making it possible to bathe the baby on a table or kitchen counter by the sink. The second style of tub is a small, plastic tub, usually with a square of sponge on the bottom and a removable suspended plastic sheet on top, on which the baby can be placed during bathing (Century's Baby Bath and Peterson's Delux Bathtub). This tub can also be used on tables or counters. As a child gets older, it will also be possible to use this tub in a regular bathtub by first making holes for drains at the front base of the tub and placing it on a nonslip mat in the regular bathtub. The child can be positioned sitting or reclining in the smaller tub. A portable hose handshower can be attached to the faucet and used in washing the child. This type of arrangement allows the child to maintain his balance while sitting in a pool of water, making it easier for you to bathe him. Since the plastic tub could be cut, it would be possible to cut slits and insert straps in the back of the tub to support the child (fig. 11). Also available on the commercial market is a small plastic chair made by Century Products with suction cups on the legs, a sponge covered seat, and a strap around the seat to hold the child in a sitting position. This chair can be used in a bathtub to support the child while bathing.

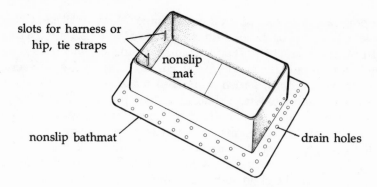

slots for harness or
hip, tie straps

nonslip
mat

nonslip bathmat

drain holes

Fig. 11.   Modified bathtub

Substitutions for commercial baby bathtubs include large plastic or enamel wash tubs, or a child's swimming tube with a plastic center in which holes can be cut for the child's legs.

Dressing
Adaptations which can be made in dressing relate either to techniques for teaching your child how to dress or to simple alterations which can be made in clothing to make dressing easier. Information on how to teach your child to dress and on positions which will make dressing easier for your child and you, when dressing him, is best obtained from your child's teacher or therapist. Below is a list of hints for choosing and adapting clothing to make dressing easier.

- loose clothing will not restrict movement
- tops with raglan sleeves allow more room for movement than tops with set-in sleeves
- V-neck or tank top T-shirts and tops are easier to pull on and off than crew neck or round neck shirts
- slip over dresses, such as jumpers or pinafores, are easier to pull on and take off than dresses with zippers or buttons
- pants with elastic waistbands are easier to learn to put on independently than pants with zippers and buttons
- flair pants allow more room for children who wear leg braces
- socks with elastic tops, like crew socks or tube socks, are easier to put on and maintain their shape longer
- small elastic loops attached to the inside top of socks make it easier for a child to grasp and pull socks on

- a strip of oilcloth glued to the inside back of a shoe may make it easier to put the shoe on
- buckles on shoes can be modified by having a shoe man add a Velcro strip under the buckle for children who have difficulty buckling their shoes
- tie shoes with hooks are easier to lace than tie shoes with eyelets
- vertical button holes are easier to button than horizontal button holes
- buttons sewn so they stand up and away from the material are easier to button than those sewn flat against the material
- buttons which are of a contrasting color to the shirt, pants, or dress are easier for the child to see when he tries to button them
- snaps are easier than buttons to fasten
- large fastenings (buttons, snaps, zippers, hooks) are easier for a child to manipulate than small fastenings
- a zipper, with an added pull tab, will be easier for a child to grasp
- Velcro dots, squares, or strips can be used to replace all fastenings for children who do not have enough fine motor control to manipulate fastenings

For more detailed information on how to adapt clothing for handicapped children, see *Self-Help Clothing for Handicapped Children* by Clari Bare, Eleanor Boettke, and Neva Waggoner which is available through the National Easter Seal Society for Crippled Children and Adults, 2023 West Ogden Avenue, Chicago, Illinois 60612.

Transporting
Car Seats.   Automobile crashes are the number one killer of young children in the United States. You can give protection to yourself and to your family in case of an automobile accident through the use of safety restraints. (See page 45 for a list of tested restraint devices.)

Automobiles come equipped with safety belts which are fine for adults and children weighing over forty or fifty pounds. However, infants, toddlers, and preschoolers require a different protection until they are large enough to use safety belts and later, after the child is over fifty-five inches tall, shoulder belts.

Holding a baby on your lap does not protect him in an automobile crash. The force from a crash multiplies the child's weight ten or twenty times, as reported in the June, 1977, issue of *Consumer Reports*.

The best protection available for your child is to put him in a restraint seat which has passed a *dynamic test*, because only this type of device can give good protection (meeting Federal Motor Vehicle Safety Standard 213 does not mean it has passed a dynamic test). When shopping for a restraint seat, take a listing of approved restraints which have passed the dynamic test and take your child with you. Before making a purchase, consider the following:

1. Does the restraint fit in your type of car? Read the instructions carefully to determine if the restraint can be properly used in your model car and with the type of seats in your car.
2. Does the device seem simple to use? Consider installation instructions because the device will only be safe if it is firmly anchored and if all buckles are properly fastened. Consider its transferability from car to car if more than one car will be used for transporting your child.
3. How well does it support your handicapped child? Some devices are designed for children who can sit alone. Try your child in the device to see if he has enough motor control for the device to be used safely.

Strollers and Carriages.   Umbrella strollers have become very popular over the past several years and, in general, are good strollers for handicapped children. For children who are too large for regular umbrella strollers, a special stroller, the Pogon Buggy by Genac, Inc., can be used. This stroller is lightweight, foldable, and can be used for children the size of a four-year-old or older until he weighs from 125 to 140 pounds.

Considerations which should be given to selecting a carriage include its overall strength and durability. If your child is severely handicapped, the carriage may be needed for several years as he grows to be of toddler and preschool size. A major disadvantage of a full-sized carriage is the difficulty of getting it into cars and on buses.

Other transporting equipment includes specialized chairs for handicapped children and adults. Most of these chairs are wheelchairs; however, there are specially designed chairs for young children with motor problems. (Major companies which deal with this type of equipment are listed on page 46). Prior to selecting any equipment of this nature, consult with a therapist or physician as to the type of equipment which will best suit your child's needs and your needs.

As a parent of a handicapped child, you may not always be aware of the various commercial products, adaptations of regular equipment, and items which can be constructed from common materials found around the house. This chapter has listed and described many of these items. If you have further questions, seek help from a therapist, special education teacher, or pediatrician.

The following is reprinted with the permission of the Michigan Office of Highway Safety Planning.

As of August 16, 1977, this is a complete list of all the restraint devices which have passed dynamic tests conducted by the University of Michigan Highway Safety Research Institute or by the Calspan Corporation. An updated list is available from the Michigan Office of Highway Safety Planning, Lansing, Michigan, 48913.

The best restraint for you is the one which suits your child's size and weight, can be used in your vehicle, and is simple and convenient to use. Try it before you buy it.

Tested Restraint Devices

For Infants only (from birth to 20 pounds), $17 to $24:

> Dyn-O-Mite by Infantseat
> Infant Love Seat by General Motors

Convertible for Infants and Toddlers, $25 to $50:

	Bobby-Mac 2 in 1 by Collier-Keyworth
	Bobby-Mac Deluxe by Collier/Keyworth
T*	Care Seat # 986 by Kantwet-Questor
CB*	Sweetheart II by Bunny Bear
	Safety Shell # 75 by Peterson
	* TravL Guard by Century
T*	Wee Care # 597 by Strolee

For Toddlers only (from when they can sit alone until they weigh 40 or 50 pounds), $12 to $50:

T/CB*	Infantseat Harness by Questor
T/CB*	Little Rider Harness by Rose Mfg.

T*	Care Seat # 885 by Kantwet/Questor
T*	Child Love Seat by General Motors
T*	Motor Totor by Century
T*	Peterson 68
	Positest by Hedstrom
T*	Swyngomatic Safety Seat by Swyngomatic/Graco
T*	Teddy Tot Astroseat V by International Mfg.
CB*	Mopar Child Seat by Chrysler Corp.
CB*	Tot Guard by Ford Motor Co.

T*	These devices have a top strap which must be pulled tight or the device is rendered unsafe.
CB*	These devices must be used in the center of the back seat.
WARNING:	An improperly used restraint may not protect your child. Read and follow carefully the directions for installation and use.

Equipment Manufacturers

Manufacturers of Commercial Equipment for Infants and Children

Century Products
2150 W. 114th St.
Cleveland, OH 44102

Cosco Company
2525 State St.
Columbus, IN 47201

Peterson Company
6904 Tujunga Ave.
North Hollywood, CA 91605

Tommee Tippee
800 North Mitchell Rd.
Newbury Park, CA 91320

Manufacturers of Special Equipment

AAMED, Inc.
1215 S. Harlem Ave.
Forest Park, IL 60130

Catalogue is available upon request. Company has a separate catalogue of equipment for children. Products include: wheelchairs, relaxation and transportation chairs, walking aids, and self care equipment.

Abbey Rents & Sells
13500 S. Figueroa
Los Angeles, CA 90061
(800-421-1170)

Catalogue is available upon request. Range of products includes: walking aids, wheelchairs, self care equipment, and developmental aids.

Adaptive Therapeutic Systems, Inc.
162 Ridge Road
Madison, CT 06443

Catalogue is available upon request. Company makes equipment for the multiply handicapped child including the Mancino Learning Center (chair for multiply handicapped), Body Harness, The Enabler (head controlled pointer), Two-Step Eater & The Pully Eater, The Communicator, The Table Writer, and The Developmental Crawler.

Cleveland Orthopedic Company
3957 Mayfield Ave.
Cleveland, OH 44121

Catalogue is available upon request. Full range of equipment for handicapped people including rehabilitation, special education, and self-care equipment.

Fred Sammons, Inc.
Box 32
Brookfield, IL 60513

Catalogue is available upon request. Specializes in self-care aids.

Genac, Inc.
2220 Norwood Ave.
Boulder, CO 80302

Makes Pogon buggy. Information available upon request.

J. A. Preston Corporation
71 Fifth Ave.
New York, NY 10003

Catalogue is only available to professionals. Company has a complete range of rehabilitation and special education equipment.

Maddak, Inc.
Industrial Road
Pequannock, NJ 07440

Catalogue is available upon request. Range of equipment includes self-care aids and some children's chairs.

Mulholland & Associates
1563 Los Angeles Ave.
Ventura, CA 93003

Information on products is available upon request. Company makes the Mulholland Growth Guidance Chairs which range from child to junior adult sizes.

Ortho-Kinetics
P.O. Box 2000 JOT 106
Waukesha, WI 53186

Catalogue is available upon request. Company makes Care Chairs (adaptive wheelchairs) for children and wheelchairs.

Rehabilitation Equipment, Inc.
1556 Third Ave.
New York, NY 10028

Company manufactures the Responder Chair (chair for the multiply handicapped child for positioning and transporting) and the Supporta Bather.

Commercial and Improvised Feeding Equipment

Commercial	Improvised
Long handled utensils (regular-sized utensils with extra long handles)	Sundae or iced tea spoons with long handles and small bowls
Child's long-handled spoon (Oneida) with a small bowl	Extend regular utensil handle length by taping popsicle sticks to handle
Built-up utensils with hard plastic or foam around handles to make them wider	Wrap and tape foam rubber around utensil handle
	Attach a utensil to a firm hair roller by weaving it over and under the wire form
	Wrap modeling clay around the handle
Bent spoons or angled spoons	Bend household spoons to the desired angle
Plastic coated or "soft-bite" spoons, especially good for children who bite on spoons during feeding	
Offset spoons with shallow bowls and flat ends; good for children with difficulty getting food off spoon with their lips	Teaspoon measuring spoon
Swivel spoons (Pace: Sta-level Training Spoon); the child does not have to rotate his wrist to keep utensil level	

The Family as
a Resource

JANE and LARRY PETERSON

There's a Child in the World

Our joy turned to grief after the birth of our first child, a son, when we learned that he had been born with Down's syndrome (Trisomy 21). While we were still groping to understand all the implications, we resolved to give Doug as rich a life as was possible within whatever limitations developed. We reasoned that whatever Doug's developmental capacity, it would be more difficult for him to achieve his potential without stimulation and enrichment.

When Doug was six months old, we began to search for a program that would guide us and give him a "head start." We found an early intervention program in which we participated for three years.

When Doug was about nine months old, we enrolled in a diaper-swim class at the YMCA, where we met another mother and her nonhandicapped infant son. We often got together for lunch and to let the boys play. That was the beginning of Doug's involvement with our local YMCA. Before I enroll him in each class, I discuss the situation and my goals for Doug with the instructor, and together we find the most appropriate age-level grouping and activity. At one point, I found that classes I had scheduled for him (painting and cooking) required too much sitting. With the staff's help, our scheduling for the next session involved more variety and included a gym period which worked beautifully.

I have found that periodically discussing the situation with the instructors gives me feedback and allows them to have a better understanding of my child. During these talks, the instructors feel free to ask questions when trying to solve a problem, and we have been able to work together. It is not that a young special child's needs are so different, but Doug often comes in contact with teachers or others who have never worked with a handicapped child and who feel awkward or have questions. Most likely the same people would feel confident handling the same problem with a nonhandicapped child. For instance, Doug was taking toys from other children, and when I asked his instructor how things were going, she mentioned the problem. I do not know how long she would have waited to mention it if I had not asked. We talked about how we handled the situation at home and I checked with Doug's nursery school to see what they did. We solved the problem together.

When Doug was two years old, he participated in a preschool laboratory, part of a university elementary education laboratory for student observation. He was the only handicapped child among fifteen normal children and it was a thoroughly enjoyable experience. Mothers attended with their children and I could see just how like other children our son was. Until then, the only groups Doug participated in were an early intervention program, with other special children, and our church nursery which I couldn't really observe. He had all the same interests as the other children, loved the cooking experiences, the painting, music, story time, and other activities. His speech was obviously delayed, and he was less adept at putting pegs in the board and at other projects which required fine motor coordination; but at that age, there was such a wide range of development and interest among the normal two-year-olds that Doug was just part of the group. Also the children played individually rather than together, so he could participate or not as he chose, watch other children, and model their actions.

When Doug was two-and-one-half years old, several mothers and I formed a weekly play group as an outgrowth of our experience at the preschool laboratory. We met at a different house each week for the next two years. As the children grew older, they began to play together, rather than side by side, and to form closer friendships. This was a difficult period for Doug, who was less creative and less skilled. He didn't play on the same level as the other children, and, although he had always enjoyed observing, he also wanted to participate. He would try to join in by taking a toy that was being used in play or by trying to help build a tower, more often than not causing it to topple. This naturally disturbed the normal playmates and frustrated Doug. The nonhandicapped playmates, however, also exhibited a range of personalities and levels of cooperation. One child was aggressive, one shy, and two were in the middle. Of course, there were altercations among the normal children. However, they did get along together more often than did Doug. I discussed our situation with the other playgroup mothers, and only the one with the shy son was disturbed by Doug's behavior. It did seem that when Doug was frustrated, he took it out on the quiet child. Eventually, we dissolved meeting as a group. Doug and I met only with the children in the group with whom Doug got along better. I was quite upset that this was necessary, but it is something that could also have happened in a group of normal playmates.

When Doug turned three, we anticipated the arrival of our second child. We decided to enroll him in a preschool program several months before the baby's birth, so he could adjust to school before the baby's arrival. The question was, which preschool program? We were fortunate to have an excellent public, special education preschool program available to us and a variety of normal nursery schools. I made appointments and observed approximately twelve programs, ranging from very structured to nonstructured approaches. An early intervention program staff had surveyed local nursery schools and collected descriptive information on facilities, programs, and staffing patterns. A program staff member assisted in my search. Our most difficult decision was whether to send Doug to the public school special education program or to a normal nursery school. In the special education program, Doug would receive special programming, individual attention, and speech therapy; he would also have a variety of consultants available. On the other hand, Doug would probably be receiving most of his later education in special education classes, and now was the time he would be most like other children. We felt that if and when the time came for him to learn subject matter, he would do so in a special education class, but our goals for preschool were socialization, enjoyment, and modeling from normal children. Since Doug had to grow up and cope in a normal world, he might as well have exposure to normal children for as long as it was possible.

We therefore selected a private preschool with a program that combines structure with free time, has an agreeable physical layout, a good staff-student ratio, and a very warm, loving staff. This school has met our needs beautifully and has worked with us most cooperatively. Initially, the Early Intervention Project staff observed Doug at school and participated on a consultation basis, setting goals for him at school. Doug was not completely toilet trained, but the school did not feel that this was a problem. Perhaps peer involvement would help train him. I do not know exactly what the turning point was, but he is now toilet trained. For a while we loaned the school a potty seat that was like the one Doug used at home, so there would be continuity. Eventually, he wanted to go to the toilet the way the other boys did.

The school staff and I have worked together to deal with problems as they arise, and now that Doug has attended for two years, there do not seem to be many problems. The school is licensed as a nursery school but maintains day care hours and is open all day. Children attend morning or afternoon sessions, or all day. The staff found that Doug's best time is early in the morning (he attends the morning session only), about eight o'clock and before most of the children arrive. He can spend time with a favorite teacher and interact in small groups where he performs best. The level of activity and noise increases with the number of children, and larger groups of children seem to overwhelm Doug. He enjoys them, but he participates less and observes more. Now that we know his most direct and satisfying interaction is early in the morning, we've made it a point to take him at that time.

The staff has always encouraged Doug to bring in items for weekly "show and tell," and we have always tried to provide him with something that he is already enthusiastic about. On some mornings, his show-and-tell leader prompts him and asks him questions about his item. We are, of course, grateful for their extra interest and help.

I have regular meetings with the staff, something they encourage all parents to do, and our exchanges are very helpful. I can understand when they are feeling frustrated, and I try to explain what it is like for a child like Doug—how it must feel to attempt something over and over again, like building a block structure or making yourself understood. Simple tasks that come easily to most children require real effort for a handicapped child, and I have to admire the stick-to-it-iveness and determination that make him face each day with his happy smile. It is not as though he fails and doesn't realize; he is intelligent and sensitive enough to feel a great sense of disappointment. This is not to say that Doug should be treated differently from other children; we have encouraged the staff to enforce the same rules with him as with the others.

Doug is now four and attends nursery school three mornings a week, the YMCA one morning, and on Tuesday mornings a neighbor and I take our children to the library for story hour, something we all enjoy. The library offers a great combination of stories, finger plays, and songs accompanied by guitar. The children's eyes shine, and we all grace either McDonald's or each other's homes for lunch afterwards.

While Doug gets along with most of the children in the neighborhood, there is one boy a year younger than Doug who bullies him. We used to feel it would be overprotective to keep Doug in our yard, away from this other child. We also felt that Doug would learn coping measures when exposed to this boy. After two years, however, we feel it best to preserve Doug's ego. We monitor the backyard play and are especially attentive when the other boy is outside; or, we keep Doug in our yard when they are both outside. Conversations with the child's mother have been ineffective.

While most of the children in our neighborhood have their close friendships, they all play individually with Doug from time to time, and frequently all the children play in a group in the backyard. We get together with neighbors who are close friends and their children during the week for coffee and to let the children play. Several of us trade babysitting with each other's children.

Our children always go on vacation with us. Doug loves the water and is quite cautious around it. He has a pair of ice skates and enjoys skating with us in the winter. Local children's concerts, especially those featuring "Tubby the Tuba," are frequent Sunday afternoon delights for Doug.

We lunch out from time to time and frequently have supper at a family restaurant. Doug orders his own meal and is proud that he is understood. His request never varies: hamburger or fried fish, french fries, and cola, which we occasionally can modify to milk. But he surprised us last week. He was looking at the menu which was illustrated with colorful samples of the fare. When his turn came to order, he asked for chicken soup, french fries, and Coke (lovely combination). We were surprised that rather than ordering by rote, he had "read" the menu and found something that appealed to him.

With Doug's continuous exposure to people in general and familiarity with a few specific children, he has stopped taking toys away from others unless he is uncomfortable in the situation. He is feeling more confident and maturing a bit. We have encountered stumbling blocks due both to our son and other people along the way; we have been hurt sometimes and do not expect this hurt to disappear in the future. Exposure to others is also exposure to difficulty and disappointment, but gradually Doug is learning to participate in a normal world. Hopefully, the normal world is learning something too.

SARA L. BROWN

Parents Have the Right

Even the parent who has gained the knowledge and skills to competently treat his child in the early years must at some point become the secondary treatment giver. In our culture the change most often occurs when the child enters the state educational system, usually kindergarten. Recent theory in attachment and separation of parent and child seems to support this separation as being healthy for both parent and child. By the age of five or six the child is generally ready to accept different adult styles and adult figures. The separation from parents of the moderately and severely handicapped child, however, is less distinct. The child may not be able to express autonomy, such as the two-year-old who can say no or run away from his parent, because he may be unable to vocalize or ambulate. His development may be greatly delayed and inconsistent across the several areas of development. Also, it may be more difficult for a parent of a handicapped child to separate due to pity, sheltering, and other protective instincts. Nonetheless, it has been my experience that especially parents of severely handicapped children are ready to entrust their children to another's care, for portions of the day, when the children have reached the age of three to four years.

It is often a welcome relief for the parent to surrender his child to another treatment giver (day-care mother, teacher, or therapist). That parent may have spent virtually every waking, and many sleeping, hour with his handicapped child and be ready for someone to relieve him, albeit for just a few hours a day. However, this time is a critical period and may determine how the parent will involve himself in future responsibilities for training his child. He may withdraw himself completely, or, after a brief spell of relief, he

57

may continue to maintain control and involvement in his child's program.

The latter response will be fostered by professionals who realize the importance of parent involvement throughout the child's life. Parents have not completed their competency training until they have become aware of the ever-increasing needs their child will have as he grows to be a school-aged, puberty-aged, legal-aged adult, still highly dependent upon his family for planning his on-going educational and vocational training. It is important to begin dealing with such issues early. Few parents are able to conceptualize their child's future when he is an infant. They are only able to cope on a day-to-day or week-to-week basis. Other parents can, at least intellectually, anticipate future problems and begin planning for their solutions. The mother who stated, "We must be watchful advocates for our children," seemed aware of tomorrow and its needs, rather than simply the needs of the day. Professionals must take an active role in preparing parents for the complexity of future problems.

There are basic rights that parents have or can be given to foster their growth in the advocacy role.

Parents have the right to be respected as competent members of the treatment team. First, and foremost, professionals must have respect for parents. The attitude the professional has toward the parent will, in great measure, affect how that parent carries out his responsibility and commitment to his handicapped child's program. If the professional has doubts about the parent, or is not tolerant of the parent's limitations or style, his attitudes will be reflected in the parent's own feelings of competency and worth.

Granted there are parents who are not going to respond to positive respect or who do not even want their child, but by far, this type of parent is a rare breed. Professionals who say, "The parents I work with just don't care about their kids," have not taken a good look at the effects their own attitudes have on parental commitment.

Just as children represent a variety of developmental levels, so do parents. They may be novices in parenting skills, as all professionals were initially new to their fields of endeavor. Just as children may reach plateaus, so do parents. Changes are not wrought overnight, but through time—over a period of years. Parents must be allowed time to develop their skills and competencies.

It makes good sense that if a professional expects a parent to become totally involved in his child's program, that parent must be allowed to participate at all levels of programming. He has the right to observe any evaluations of his child. He has the right to read the records of those evaluations. He has the right, and indeed the responsibility, to ask questions of those evaluators to clarify his understanding of his child's needs and strengths.

Because it is the ultimate responsibility of the parent to seek and coordinate services for his child, to serve as an agency liaison, and to anticipate future problems, the parent must be recognized as a legitimate contributor. He is the only constant and permanent member of his child's treatment team.

Parents have the right to knowledge over time. Parents must be informed. If they are to have any control over the decisions which affect their family unit, parents must have access to information and resources available in their community. It is the responsibility of the community and professionals to publicize this information.

It is the responsibility of the doctors involved to explain the child's diagnosis and prognosis to the family in terms that they can understand. Such explanations may be required many times. It is the responsibility of the school evaluator or caseworker to explain the meaning of evaluation results to parents in terms they can understand. It is the responsibility of the state and local community to make known the legislated rights of the handicapped child. It is the responsibility of each professional who works with a family to inform them of their rights and their responsibility to take advantage of those rights.

Both parents and professionals should be aware and knowledgeable of the Education for All Handicapped Children Act of 1975 (Public Act 94–142) and their own state mandates. They can be aware by writing their state department of Education and the U.S. Department of Health, Education, and Welfare, Department of Education, for the *Education of Handicapped Children and Incentive Grants Program Register.* Also, some states hold open hearings on the subjects of educational rights for the handicapped, state-appealed cases, and new considerations for legislation. Parents and professionals should keep themselves informed by reading their local newspapers and calling the local education association, the local or intermediate school district, or parent advocacy organizations, such as the Association for Retarded Citizens, Association for Children with Learning Disabilities, Parent Advisory Council, and others.

Essentially, Public Law 94–142 mandates states to submit plans to the U.S. Department of Health, Education, and Welfare for the full education of handicapped children between the ages of three and eighteen by 1979, and three and twenty-one by 1980. (There are grant incentives for states to provide services to children below the age of three.) These plans must describe educational programs based on evaluation findings for all types of handicapped children. In the state of Michigan, local school districts are mandated to provide services for children between the ages of birth and twenty-five as determined by evaluations and decisions made at the yearly Educational Planning and Placement Committee (EPPC) meeting. These meetings are attended by representatives of the diagnostic team, local and intermediate school district personnel, and parents. At the EPPC, an individualized program is completed and a contract is signed by the professionals and parents. Parents may refuse to sign the contract if they feel the school district is not attempting to offer appropriate services to the child.

Resources vary from community to community and state to state. It is often very difficult for parents to become aware of available resources. Professionals should connect parents with resources appropriate to the parents' current needs. At the same time, the parent should always be a seeker and do as much of the resource searching as he is able. How this information is given is as important as what is said. As everyone knows, most professionals could polish up their bedside manners. There seem to be several guidelines which parents themselves have suggested to professionals:

1. The parent will prompt a professional by asking questions. The questions should be answered directly and truthfully. Parents generally ask questions to which they need answers. If we answer the questions they ask, rather than filling in what we want them to know, they will generally be better able to receive the information.
2. None of us processes new information 100 percent efficiently. It is more difficult to process information which is contrary to our belief system or to our plans and goals. When a parent who has looked forward to the birth or growth of a child is told that the child is less than perfect, how difficult it must be for him to go beyond processing that one piece of cognitive dissonance. One set of parents

said it should be done simply by asking the parent, "What do you want to know?"

3. Professionals must learn to sense the nonverbal cues which parents give. When we become aware that parents do not have to put their hands over their ears to block out words which hurt, we will be ready to watch for signs of tolerance. Facial expression, eye contact, sitting positions, and voice control are all signs for the professional to read.

An important thing for the professional to remember is that bad news must be digested over a period of time. Many parents cannot take everything at one blow. One mother of a Down's syndrome child was invited to talk to a new mother whose child also had the syndrome. In her eagerness to help, she showed a picture of her older Down's child to the new mother. She soon realized that was a mistake. The new mother was not ready to accept the visible characteristics as someday belonging to her child.

Some professionals take parents of retarded infants on tours of local retardation centers to show them what is available in the community and to desensitize them. This has often been a mistake for parents who have not had time to work through their initial resentment, denial, and guilt. They cannot handle the visible experience of seeing the older children and the complexity of their handicaps.

Parents have the right to know all the options. Too often decisions affecting a handicapped child are made by professionals with little regard for the priorities or circumstances of the family itself. Problem-solving dialogue between the family and the professional should help both parties arrive at a mutual decision. The doctor who feels that a child needs braces rather than corrective surgery should have a meeting with the family to discuss all of the available options. The advantages of each option will be discussed and weighed, with everyone taking part in the responsibility for making the decision.

Similarly, the professional who may have a bias toward one therapeutic method over another (behavioral management versus play therapy) should also inform the family of the options available to them, again discussing reasons behind decisions. In this way, families become realistic about the nature of treatment options. Parents who receive information concerning differences in theories are better able to cope with differing opinions in years to come.

Again, in the early years, it is their commitment that is so necessary to the proposed changes and growth of the child.

In the educational system, staffing conferences and parent informings must be held with parents and professionals discussing available options. In Michigan, the EPPC meetings serve this function. At these meetings, parents learn of the program options for their child; they have the opportunity to ask questions about these programs; and they make requests for other services. It is recommended that parents take an advocate with them, such as another parent, a professional who knows their child well, or a professional advocate from a local organization such as the Association for Retarded Citizens. The advocate serves to draw out all the available options, press for additional services, and clarify any ambiguities. A programming contract is then drawn up, and parents may sign or refuse to sign it.

Parents have the right to help set programming priorities for their child. Although professionals working with a child may have certain long-range goals for that child, their respect for parental priorities will often temper immediate program goals. Each family is a unique unit. It has its own set of dynamics which culminates in unique needs and complexities. Many families are under financial or emotional stress, or they may have medical or supportive needs which are not being met. The priorities a family has are generally based on these needs. Filling these needs may ease family stress. Parents of a large number of children may not be able to take time to toilet train a handicapped child until a later date. Acting-out behaviors often provoke families to interact negatively on a daily basis with the child, and nothing is accomplished until those behaviors are eliminated. While climbing up and down steps may be a high priority with the professional, the parent may be concerned about the safety of the steps available in the home.

During the initial program-planning sessions, professionals can prompt parents to verbalize their priorities by asking them: "What would make your life easier?" Parents respond with a variety of answers depending on their child's own handicap and family circumstances. Many respond, "If I could just get him to quit banging his head!" or, "If we could eliminate his temper tantrums!" Others see independence in feeding or ambulation as a priority which would free other family members from additional responsibilities. A professional who heeds this call for help and initiates appropriate programming is well on his way toward earning credibility with parents. If a parent learns that his own priorities are important, he is more willing to begin to understand the priorities which the professional has for the child.

Family situations and the child's type of handicap also determine the degree of programming necessary. A single parent, or parents with large families, may need more relief from a severely impaired or a behaviorally involved child. Such children may be programmed far more consistently in a preschool setting for several hours a day. A parent who wants to keep his child at home, however, should be given home programming guidance to maximize his child's environment.

Parent participation in program and priority planning sessions not only allows for increase in trust between the professional and the parent, but also assures parental carry-over at home. Professionals working with children know how difficult it is to achieve goals if the goals are not carried through at home. For children under the developmental age of three or four, parent commitment is critical. Parents are by far the major influence over the child at this time. Their daily care, handling, and interaction may be critical features in the growth and development of the handicapped child. The more severely involved the child is, the more necessary parent commitment becomes. Daily physical handling of the cerebral palsied child is of critical importance, as is consistent emotional handling of the emotionally impaired child. A severely retarded child may sleep constantly if not awakened and stimulated out of his apathy. Such children will seldom benefit in a program which bypasses the parent.

Parents have the right to advocate without fear of ostracism. Parents can become marked. A parent who becomes a familiar face in the school, clinic, hospital, or political setting is a threat to the status quo and is perceived as a threat to many professionals. Such parents are labeled troublemakers and their opinions, no matter how valid, are looked upon with disdain. (On the other hand, some parents tear into a system like lions, without stopping to consider how changes might best be wrought. They alienate those who could make changes by impatiently going directly to the top.)

It is time for mutual problem solving in changing the educational, medical, and support systems. Systems which deal with parents should include parent representatives in decision-making sessions. Parents who seek services for themselves and their children should be willing to bear partial responsibility by recognizing that changes are made only over time.

Parents should not have to feel guilty because they seek two-week respite care for the sake of their family's mental health, or two-year placement for their child when they have come to the end of their own resources. Families should not have to feel guilty for seeking a second medical or diagnostic opinion. Parents should not be made to feel guilty when they disagree with professionals regarding programming priorities the family feels are burdensome.

Neither should parents have to beg for services due them through legislation, or their basic rights as human beings to health and happiness. Parents should be free to seek help from all sources and to exhaust all avenues of service without alienating those in the services they seek.

Parents have the right to withdraw their efforts. Just as parents have the right to shape and direct their child's treatment, so have they the right to withdraw their commitment in times of stress and crisis. There are times when the health of the family is dependent on a de-emphasis of the handicapped child's needs.

When a family finds out their handicapped child is dying, they may begin a withdrawal process that is mentally healthy. A preparation for death in the family may depend on normalizing the child by ignoring the handicap, or by spending less therapeutic time, which is indicative of hope for the future. Families of handicapped children have a right to prepare for a death in the same way as families with normal children. They generally want to spend as much time as possible as a family unit without intruders.

There are times when the emotional stress of having a handicapped child, coupled with the complexity of daily living problems, is more than a family can bear. Families are generally aware of their own coping tolerance and should be allowed to say "I cannot cope anymore." If there are other medical or financial problems which must first be taken care of, then help for the child may have to wait until the family has again pooled its resources for the special child. In the meanwhile, professionals can remain at a safe distance, offering support whenever possible.

At the present time, many professionals would like to strike the word *institutionalization* out of common usage, and not only the word, but the concept the word represents as well. There are times when intact families reach the point of emotional and physical exhaustion; a point when the family cannot cope with the constant needs of the handicapped child. A mother with severe backaches may no longer be able to carry her fifty-pound, nonambulatory child in and out of the house. Another family does not sleep for more than two hours at a time because the child cries constantly during the night. A single parent may not be able to cope with the emotional strain of raising and caring for a multiply handicapped child and other children in the family. A child who needs ongoing medical care such as intravenous feedings, lung suctioning, postural drainage, and catheterization may exhaust a family's coping tolerance to the point of dividing the family. During the times of inner resource depletion, families should be able to ask for foster or institutional care without feeling they are giving up or rejecting their child. Sensitive professionals must help ease the family guilt at these times through tolerance and empathy.

Parents have the right to legal recourse when due process has been violated. Recent litigation hearings (lawsuits) before the Supreme Court have determined that the 14th Amendment guarantees the right of an individual to an education. This amendment guarantees the right to life, liberty, and property. The court reasoned that potential earning power (e.g., to obtain property) is deprived if the individual is denied the right to an education. This amendment also guarantees the individual the right to equal protection under the law. Therefore, parents can appeal on the basis of the 14th Amendment if their child has been deprived of an education (Williams, 1977).

The recent federal mandate, Public Law 94–142, 1975, guarantees the right to an education to handicapped children. Parents can appeal if they feel this right has been violated. Litigation appeals, however, are expensive. They involve hiring a lawyer who has an interest and background in special education, and diagnosticians who will support the case based on their evaluative findings. Many of these appeals become tied up in the courts and are not decided for several years. They are time and resource consuming. These appeals, however, have served as a motivating force for school systems to improve existing programs and to develop new ones.

There is another form of recourse called *arbitration*. This type of hearing includes representatives from the local and intermediate school districts, the parents, and an agreed-upon third party moderator who discusses the grievances and works toward a solution. The purpose of the arbitration is to solve problems within the local setting while avoiding the expense and time lapse of litigation hearings. It also serves as an opportunity for calling in a second opinion and bargaining for services (Beekman, 1977).

This chapter has been concerned with parents' rights, but a right usually carries with it a responsibility. Leo Cain, an educator who has worked with parent groups a number of years, speaks of parents banding together as "a significant force at national, state and local levels." He credits parents with having a major influence in the establishment of special schools for the handicapped, changes in legislation to improve special educational services, funding at the national level for research and service grants, and advocacy for the handicapped through groups and litigation (Cain, 1976). These changes were not achieved overnight or without a tremendous effort by parents who recognized not only their rights and the rights of their children, but their responsibility for assuring the provision of these rights.

References

Beekman, L. 1977. Presentation at The Impact and Implications of State and Federal Laws Affecting Handicapped Individuals May Conference, Ann Arbor, Michigan.

Cain, L. F. 1976. "Parent Groups: Their Role in a Better Life for the Handicapped," *Exceptional Children* May, pp. 432–37.

Williams, J. 1977. Presentation at The Impact and Implications of State and Federal Legislation Affecting Handicapped Individuals May Conference, Ann Arbor, Michigan.

Siblings Have the Right

The following open letter is written for brothers and sisters of the handicapped with the hope that they will become more understanding and active. Concern for siblings of the handicapped has often been neglected by both parents and professionals. Support and counsel for them is seldom available. It is hoped that siblings themselves will begin organizing in groups for their mutual support.

Dear Friend:

So you have a brother or sister who is different? Your friends call your sister a "retard" or your brother a "cripple"? You are asking, "Why did this happen to me?"

If you answered yes to any of these questions, you're probably feeling sorry for yourself, and you have that right --for a little while. All people feel sorry for themselves and for a handicapped person once in awhile. But feeling sorry for yourself much of the time does not help. "Sorry" does not change things much. "Sorry" does not improve a handicap either.

There is something you can do to help yourself and your brother or sister. You can learn to understand. Ask your parents questions such as: "What does mental retardation mean?" or "Will my sister always be crippled?" or "Will my brother ever learn to talk?" Ask your teacher and your brother's or sister's special teachers about what is wrong and what that means for you and your family. You have a right to know. Learn all you can. As you truly begin to learn, you will begin to understand.

You will understand why Mom gets tired after lifting a heavy brother or sister who cannot walk yet, day after day. You will understand why Dad is more worried. (Special equipment or training costs money, and he may be concerned about paying for it.) You will begin to understand why Mom and Dad don't spend as much time with you and why they expect you to do more to help out around the house. You may also understand why it is sometimes difficult for them to talk about handicaps. You see, all parents dream that their children will be healthy, strong, and intelligent. It is very difficult for them to understand why they have a "special" child.

There is one more thing you may be worried about: whether your brother's or sister's handicap is "catching." Sometimes other children get the idea that it's like chicken pox or a virus. But you cannot "catch" a handicap. Many handicaps are determined before a child is born or during the birth process. Others are a result of a severe disease or infection. Other handicaps can be caused by accidents.

When you talk to your friends, it's a good idea to teach them the things you've learned. If they see that you know more about your brother's or sister's handicap than they do, they may begin to ask questions because of their desire to learn and help. Some children will tease you about your special brother or sister because they don't understand. If they hear you using the words <u>retarded</u>, <u>crippled</u>, or <u>brain damaged</u> to describe your brother or sister in a realistic manner, they will no longer enjoy using these words to get on your back. If you don't get "hairy" about it, they will soon learn to understand, as you have done.

There is one more thing that you can do as you are learning to understand: talk with other kids who have handicapped brothers and sisters. Rap groups and sibling groups may not be available in your community, but why wait until they are? Organize one yourself. Visit with your brother's or sister's teachers and therapists. They can be of help in suggesting others who might join your group.

Sincerely,

Sara

Sara L. Brown

P.S. Good luck to you! You are healthy and full of life. Make the most of it. You have the right.

SALLY J. ROGERS

A Child's Evaluation –
It's a Family Affair

A few weeks ago I was talking with a mother in the process of evaluating her emotionally disturbed young son. I asked her whether her child had seen a psychologist before, and when she said yes, I asked what the psychologist had found out about him. "I don't really know," she said. "It was a bad day, the kids were screaming and hollering all the time I was on the phone, and I just couldn't think. I tried to listen to what he was saying, but it was over so fast. All I remember is he said Jimmy needed more time with his dad. And what can I do about that? I don't know what he thought was wrong with Jimmy!" The psychologist's phone conversation lasted only five minutes.

Why do some psychologists treat parents so casually? The way parents are treated in their first contacts with professionals has a tremendous influence on their attitudes and behaviors. It determines whether parents passively send their child to whatever program the professionals recommend, or whether they will request all options, examine various programs, select according to their own preference, and then accompany the child to the program. It determines whether parents sit at home on parent visiting days, or whether they will request opportunities to visit their child's program and then take an active part in the program, rather than passively viewing from the sidelines. It also determines whether parents forget the name of the professional evaluating their child ten minutes after the evaluation, or whether they write down a name and phone number and then later call to ask questions, clarify points, or report observations and information that they feel are

69

relevant. All of these options are greatly influenced by the ways in which parents are included in, or excluded from, their children's evaluations.

Evaluation as a Preview

Evaluation is frequently the first step in a child's entry into an educational program, and it provides an opportune occasion to demonstrate a commitment to parent involvement. In too many programs, the evaluation process involves the child's being whisked away and evaluated behind closed doors by a number of professionals. Meanwhile, the parents are interviewed by a social worker and must wait until the child is returned to them, with little knowledge of what went on. Perhaps this happens because professionals feel that parents will not understand the evaluation process, or that parents may become emotionally upset by watching their child's failures. It doesn't matter how the exclusion of parents began; what is important is how it can be changed.

Initial Interview

Beginning a child's evaluation with a parent or family interview serves several purposes. It provides the evaluator with a chance to see the child through the parents' eyes and to appreciate their fears, worries, and doubts about their child. It also provides a flavor of the emotional climate in which the child lives and the emotional forces which influence the child's behavior in one direction or another. The cohesiveness of the family—the strength of the marital relationship, relations with children, extended family, friends, and neighbors—is important in assessing the coping skills of the family. By uncovering the parents' expectations, fears, and hopes for their child's future, the evaluator has a chance to see the extent to which the parents understand their child's handicap. Are they denying or exaggerating the severity of the child's handicap? Are they so afraid of the implications of having a handicapped child that they cannot yet consider the future? Are they distorting their own difficulties with the child by rationalizing or by placing blame on the child, a sibling, a demanding job, or a poor marriage? Are they intellectualizing the problem or maintaining an emotional distance from the child in the process? Or, are they able to face the reality of the situation both emotionally and intellectually, without denying the pain, fear, and uncertainty, while at the same time using a problem-solving approach to seek solutions to their own questions?

For the parents, an initial interview provides an opportunity to discuss with a skilled listener the concerns which all parents have about their children, but which are greatly intensified when the child is handicapped. It can allow parents to hear each other's viewpoints and reactions to issues which they seldom discuss. A parent-centered interview communicates to parents the importance of their thoughts and feelings, rather than the view of parents as merely producers and transporters of the child; it immediately broadens the focus to the entire family. Professional attitudes toward parents as the most knowledgeable people about their child and their key role as major treatment givers are demonstrated by the importance with which the parent interview is treated. Finally, the initial interview gives the parents a preview of the staff, an opportunity to develop a relationship with one staff member, and a chance to size up how the program treats parents, what it considers important, whether the staff is made up of real people rather than just another set of professionals, and whether the program may give them some real help.

The initial interview conveys much information about the philosophy of the program staff. One of the surest giveaways of the traditional child-treatment-centered program is the parent interview which is used to gather information about the child—developmental milestones, medical history, abnormal behavior—thus focusing almost exclusively on the child. A parent- and family-centered program must convey a very different message, and that message must be communicated throughout the initial interview. Methods that convey a positive message are:

1. *Both parents (and sometimes the siblings, too) are present for the initial interview, and it is scheduled at a time when both parents can be there.*

   Thus, the message immediately conveyed is that a handicapped child is a family issue, not just an additional burden for the mother. Not only are both parents present, but the interviewer draws everyone into the conversation so that all have chances to voice their opinions. The interviewer recognizes the value of each person and prevents the dominant member from speaking for all the others, which inevitably leads to misrepresentation and asserts that some speakers are more important than others.

2. *The interview is open-ended; its purpose is to explore the family's reaction to the handicapped child—their questions, their doubts, their worries.*

The interviewer must be willing to save questionnaires and forms until another time and must allow the conversation to cover whatever topics are important to the family, asking questions which will allow each person present to voice his concerns, uncertainties, opinions, and needs. Open-ended questions such as "What is it like living with Billy?"; "What do you hope to get from us?"; and, "What went wrong that brought you here?" allow the parents to move in whatever direction they choose, with the interviewer helping them to form their thoughts.

3. *The interview is parent-centered.*

Discussion of the child does not dominate the conversation. Rather, the interviewer maintains the focus on the parents' thoughts, the parents' feelings, the parents' reactions to their child and to each other. Parents will usually take the opportunity to express their thoughts and appreciate the interviewer's interest in them. So often the parents' needs are ignored in favor of the child's needs. Occasionally parents will be uncomfortable with the focus on them. An explanation of the importance of understanding a child's family is usually enough to reassure them, and their response to this unaccustomed professional attention is excellent.

The Evaluation Itself

There is much mystique and misconception about evaluations, particularly psychological evaluations. There is no better way to bridge that gap than to make sure the parents observe the evaluation in its entirety, so that they can see the range of behaviors tested, the child's reactions, and his successes and failures. When parents observe, many of the defenses they use to cope with negative information—"He was tired," "She didn't see what he can really do," "How can someone possibly know how a baby thinks?"—are nullified, because the parents see for themselves the evaluator's competence, the child's performance, and the kinds of skills tested.

Whenever possible, parents should be in the testing room holding the child, observing from the sidelines, or helping to administer some of the early social and verbal tasks. In this way, the evaluator can explain the behaviors each task is trying to elicit; point out the child's successes; explain some of the child's failures; and model optimal ways of stimulating, positioning, and playing with the child. At the same time, activities which support emerging skills can be suggested for use at home. These suggestions tie the evaluation tasks to the child's everyday life.

In addition to parent education, there are distinct benefits to having a parent in the room during an evaluation. The evaluator has a chance to observe parent-child interactions and parent-parent interactions in a less formal situation than in the initial interview. The evaluator also has some assistance with wiggly, floppy, or very active young children, or with those children whose motor handicaps require special positioning. Finally, the parents are exposed to a more human side of the professional. When they see the psychologist make silly faces and funny noises for their child, or treat the child with affection or aggravation, some of the distance between parents and the professional is bridged.

Many professionals are uncomfortable with this idea. They feel inhibited with the parents present, or they worry about making mistakes or looking foolish in front of the parents. They do not want this much exposure. And yet it is just that opportunity to see the professional in a spontaneous, human situation, unable to hide behind a desk, a chart, or a title, that allows for the humanness to shine through. This is how the distance between parents and the professional is bridged. The professional can encourage parents to join with him and form a team by giving up artificial status differences, by sharing skills and errors, knowledge and ignorance, hopes and frustrations.

After the evaluation is completed, the evaluator can sit down with the parents to answer questions, share reactions to the evaluation, and give them a general idea of the child's performance. If the child has been difficult to test or the evaluator is confused by the results or the complicated findings, he should say so. After setting up a formal time to discuss the findings in detail, the evaluation is finished. If plenty of explanation occurred during the evaluation itself, little is needed now. If the parents observed through two-way glass or by watching a video tape, rather than participated, another professional can be with them to explain activity, answer questions, or draw their attention to important tasks. Whatever questions they have after the evaluation should be considered, but one must be able to say, "I just don't know yet; I'll try to answer that when we meet next time."

Parent Feedback Meeting
The feedback meeting is such a difficult one for many professionals that they may be tempted to depend on a social worker or psycholo-

gist to relay the findings. Yet maintaining a strong relationship between the interdisciplinary team and the family at this point is critical to all future dealings with them, because it is at this team meeting that plans for lessening the difficulties of child and family must be turned into action by the family.

How one defines the purpose of this meeting determines how well it will go. Too often the meeting is seen as the time in which the professionals tell the parents what they found and tell the parents what to do about it. Unfortunately, that is exactly what usually happens. Parents and staff sit at a table; the staff members read their individual reports, one at a time; they give their recommendations, one at a time; and one staff member summarizes, lists the recommendations, and asks if the parents have any questions. The parents seldom do. Their response to this dehumanizing experience is to leave it as quickly as possible, because there is really no place for them in that kind of meeting. It is something like sitting through a long, dry lecture filled with unfamiliar technical terms and numbers, except that it is so much worse, because it is the parent's child who is being reduced to numbers and phrases. The parents' major concerns—their feelings, worries, doubts, and need to understand—are never addressed. They do not get what they came for, and chances are, they will not come back.

A better way to view this feedback meeting is as the time when those who are vitally concerned with the child sit down together to share their thoughts and feelings about what the problems are and learn how they can join together to lessen them. A major emphasis now is on dialogue among all participants as they talk together to try to conceptualize the problems and to search for some solutions; all will share relevant information which fits this purpose. Professional jargon, monologue presentations, overbearing opinions and advice should not disrupt the flow of thoughts and ideas. The meeting should resemble a brainstorming session among a team of planners, where the people will be talking to each other about a common subject, each bringing unanswered questions as well as insights to share with the group.

This kind of parent feedback meeting models the kind of parent involvement that is sought in all aspects of an ideal program and reflects the program's basic beliefs. In this meeting, the parents become members of the team with valuable information to share and important questions to ask. Their initial role as advocate for their child is enhanced by the respect which they receive, the information that is shared with them, the decisions they are expected to make, and the support for their right to decide on whatever alternatives they choose. Their active involvement—their questions, statements, criticisms, information, opinions—is sought, heard, and honestly responded to by the professionals present. This kind of active dialogue is modeled for the parents by the professionals present.

The staff can gauge their success with a family in proportion to the active involvement the parents have throughout the evaluation and feedback process. The professionals have fulfilled their role by assisting the family to understand the child's needs and to become better able to meet those needs, while at the same time recognizing the needs within the family and helping the family to recognize and meet its own needs. Helping a family to become more responsive to its own needs is what professional intervention is all about.

MARTHA UFFORD DICKERSON and
SARA L. BROWN

A Search for a Family

The following is an interview by Sara L. Brown of Martha Ufford Dickerson, a social worker at the Institute for the Study of Mental Retardation and Related Disabilities who has participated in early intervention workshops. Mrs. Dickerson has dual credibility as an effective professional and as a foster parent for four retarded teen-aged boys.

Sara: I was curious as to how you and your husband came to the decision to be parents again. Here it is some twenty years after you have already had children of your own; they're raised for the most part; they're in college or married. What made you decide to go back to the parenting role?

Martha: It was the result of a process. I don't think that we ever just suddenly one day said, "Let's have some more children." It was a recognition over a period of time that we really enjoyed having kids in the house. We had two of our own children, and they had many friends. For about eighteen or twenty years, through their youth and high school, our house was usually filled with our children and their friends. As they began to move into their own lives in different parts of the country, we began to realize what a hole there was at home and how much we had enjoyed young people. We enjoyed being parents, and sometimes I think we regretted that we didn't have a larger family. As the years went on we began to realize we still had the energy and desire to parent more children.

77

Sara: That prompts a more relevant question. What makes people at the age of fifty decide to foster handicapped children?

Martha: Well, down through the years my husband and I had a dream of a camp for children who normally couldn't go to camp because of behavioral problems. As we learned more about ourselves, we realized that we didn't like to take care of property, so that ruled out the idea of the camp. But we still believed we had some skills that could prepare us to work with children who might be handicapped in one way or another. We thought about working with children identified as disturbed children. In 1969 I began to work in an agency that served young adults with retardation, and this influenced our decision. My husband did a lot of volunteer work with me, such as training the young people to use buses and accompanying them to football games and other normalizing activities. We began to realize that people are people and their needs are comparable regardless of what their disabilities are. So, my professional involvement influenced our decision to move in the direction of fostering children with retardation. In our professional contacts and exposure to institutions, my husband and I decided that we could provide a more homelike atmosphere than institutions were providing. To answer your question, I think it was that we needed to parent, that we believed there were other alternatives than institutions for children, and that we thought we had skills that could reach children who had disabilities. Those three components came together in time.

Sara: How did you begin? By taking one child?

Martha: We took two children at first. We felt that it would be difficult for any child to leave a situation where he had lived with literally hundreds of kids like himself and come to live with a middle-aged couple. So we brought two boys out of the institution at the same time. Ten months later the third boy joined our family, and three years later the fourth boy. We probably will not take any more, but we will continue to have these boys in our home until they are grown and have some appropriate place to live as adults in our society.

Sara: How has your work as a professional been influenced by having the retarded boys in your home, and being a parent for these children?

Martha: I believe that as a professional social worker I have developed more genuine empathy for parents who accept the challenge of raising a child with a disability. I'd like to think that I was doing a reasonable job working with parents five years ago just because I cared and wanted to be helpful to them. But I don't believe I had an understanding of what it was like to live twenty-four hours a day, seven days a week, with a child who was not meeting all of a mother's dreams. I've been fortunate; we had it both ways. Our biological children were healthy, curious, bright, challenging children so that every day was new. They learned new tasks, skills, and concepts. It was exciting to live with them. There were challenges and difficulties, but the difficulties were usually because they were inquisitive, healthy, normal kids growing up and wanting to be like, but also different from, their parents.

As a result of having the four retarded children living with us, I believe I am more in touch with what it's like to live with a child who takes a very, very long time to learn something that is as basic as toilet training. My two biological children were toilet trained by three. I don't remember a wet bed after that. It was a whole other issue with two of our four retarded boys. To toilet train a thirteen- and fifteen-year-old and to deal with wet beds when a boy is sixteen is a very different thing. I am more tuned in to what that does to a mother, father, and a family system.

So in answer to your question, I believe that working with the children has expanded my ability to empathize with a family who has a disabled child; I am able to make constructive suggestions for improving the structure and routine of their home. You see, my husband and I in our home situation are able to use, in an objective manner, many ideas from professional colleagues. I'm sure that we find it easier to incorporate those ideas from our colleagues because the boys are not our biological children. I think now that we are in a position to share those ideas with other families.

Sara: It sounds to me that you have said that even though you see your foster children more objectively, you still experience the same kinds of feelings that natural parents have toward their children: anger, guilt, frustration, and impatience. I'm sure that you have concerns about the future for your boys. How do parents deal with these feelings in a healthy way?

Martha: That's a very complicated question. I think the first thing I want to say is that it is true that we have felt all of the feelings that you have listed. Perhaps it is easier for my husband and me to allay guilt feelings because we are not the biological parents of these children. It is true that there are times when I get so frustrated with them—angry, annoyed, weary—that I find myself saying, "Why are you angry with John? He can't help that; he just cannot learn that now." Even though I understand John's limitations, my feelings are feelings of anger and frustration, and I believe that those are *OK* feelings. At home we acknowledge that a feeling is OK. It's what we *do* about our feelings that is important.

Parents must learn that it is OK to have the whole range of feelings: despair, anger, guilt, frustration, as well as joy with the child. However, it is important to be consistent in how you handle those feelings. As a parent, I have no right to act out my anger and frustration on the child. I think the best thing is to leave the situation, just remove myself until I am in better control. I don't have any qualms about saying to John or Stewart, "I am angry, and I don't want to be with you now." I think they need to learn that everyone has a range of feelings and that we do not have warm feelings all the time. I want to model for them that it is OK to be angry; it's OK to be frustrated; but I also want to model for them that I must be responsible for such feelings.

Sara: It seems to me that you have been discussing feelings that are much more outwardly expressed, feelings that we can verbalize: "I am angry with you; I'm frustrated with you." There is another feeling that we touched on and that is guilt. Guilt seems to be a more insidious feeling that creeps up on a person before he is even aware of it. He cannot express it, and maybe it doesn't go away. How can parents deal with guilt?

Martha: I think you are right when you talk about the evasiveness of guilt. We have to give parents the opportunity to talk that out as much as they are able. It's usual for parents to blame themselves for the child's disabilities. There are many common statements made by parents such as, "I really shouldn't have been pregnant anyway;" "I was into drugs;" or, "I knew that my cousin's child had learning problems." It's usual for any unresolved incidences in either parent's life to resurface, to serve as a kind of repository for the guilt, now that this child has been born. Somehow parents need to have an opportunity to reason that out alone and together, so they can look at the guilt and begin to deal with it in a rational manner. It is often comforting for parents to learn that the disability is not a result of any evil thing that they did, but is something that just happened. Unfortunately, many parents feel such heavy disappointment that it is not easy to get rid of guilt. The disappointment and despair are so heavy for them that they feel, "How could this happen to me? I must have been a very bad person; I must have done something wicked that put this load on me."

Sara: Are you saying that with help some parents can talk about and work through these feelings of guilt and despair when their child is very young and not have to deal with them the rest of their lives? Or, will these feelings crop up again when their child gets older?

Martha: Some parents are able to work this through, deal with their disappointment, pick up their lives, and establish a certain amount of stability in their individual and family worlds. These parents are able to realize that the disappointments and sadness around the disabled child are just one aspect of their life, and that there are other healthy, satisfying, fulfilling experiences happening to them. However, there are some parents who have difficulty. It has been my experience that some parents have a recurrence of the feelings of despair. It seems that some parents move toward an acceptance of the handicap during the first few years of their child's life. It's as though they come to terms with their disappointments and grief over the child. I think of it in terms of a death of a dream child. I have often thought that no parent ever dreamed of having a child other than a perfect child, a beautiful child, a talented child.

Some parents do very well accepting the death of that dream child and accept the responsibility for rearing a special child who has special demands and needs. They seem to do very well for the first four or five years. I think there are many reasons for that. The community is able to be affectively supportive to a family who has a *little* child with a disability. A disabled child is often an extremely appealing child. Universally, people seem to reach out warmly toward a little person. Everyone loves a baby, everyone loves a baby with a problem. That somehow shifts as the child grows into a teenager and then an adult. I have found that even the family that has done quite well accepting the baby is thrown into a tailspin as that child begins to grow.

I have noticed that it is not uncommon for families to be thrown into a time of despair when they realize that their child is not going to be a part of the American dream, especially traditional education. So much of how we become acculturated in America is through the public school system. Our children's lives revolve around the school house—their contacts with friends, their extra social activities, and their peer status. Much of a child's identity as a person, including the ability to move away from the family toward independence, is supported by that school experience. It is a rude shock for the family of the disabled child to realize that their child is not going to have those experiences.

Now the child, in addition to having a disability, is special in another way. He has had the identifying label as the handicapped child in a family, and now is identified as a special child within the school system. This perpetuation of dependence increases the burden at home. For example, think about normal children and how they enter the public school system, join the Scouts, join the church choir, or play down the street after school with their friends. The responsibility of parenting shifts so that mothers and fathers have more free time to pursue the development of their own individual lives. Many mothers go back to school. But all of a sudden, for the family who has the special child, the demands on the parents actually begin to increase. Parents find they also have to take special measures for their special child to receive recreational and extra-curricular services offered in the community. The gap between the child and his peer group becomes more observable; the more impaired the child is, the greater the gap. It also happens that this comes about at the time other children have such a need to be like their peers. The typical third or fourth grader is unable to reach out and be tolerant of, or friendly with, his peer who has a disability. It's almost as though children of that age are fearful that they might "catch" the difference. At the same time, parents begin to feel the isolation of their child from his peers, and this is an additional source of pain, despair, disappointment, and grief.

I would suggest though, this is not the only time that these feelings resurface. Some families survive the time of entrance into the special school situation, and some families are fortunate that they are able to build a world for their child where he has good peer contact. Some families survive nicely until their child reaches puberty. But often, when the child with a disability moves toward adolescence, another time of alienation surfaces. It's as though suddenly the parents must deal with this child as a sexual person with all the needs, interests, and concerns that any other person moving into adolescence has. However, for the person with the disability, as well as the family of such a child, there are complicating factors that are very awesome. The complexity of the problem depends upon the severity of the disability. It is a challenge to teach a daughter who is severely impaired to accomplish independently menstrual hygiene. Yet, the task has to be learned. It is a challenge for parents of a severely impaired seventeen-year-old boy to deal with the issues of masturbation. Yet they must be dealt with.

Children in the public school system have had opportunities to learn a great deal about sexuality from their friends. They have been picking up some of the ideas about the rights, responsibilities, and privileges of being a sexual person. They have observed from different models the way one relates to a person of the opposite sex, depending upon the age of that person and one's interest in him. The children with disabilities have been denied much of that rich exposure. Once again they are at a new plateau where the distance between what happens to most people and what is possible for them is dramatically increased. Suddenly parents have to deal with the issue that their child is growing up and wants to be sexually expressive. The parents have to examine their feelings about their child handling sexual experiences. Some parents have to deal with a child who, although he is having nocturnal emissions, may never be able to handle the responsibilities of parenthood.

Parents become ambivalent. On the one hand, they want their children to know the strengths that come from healthy loving and all of its forms of expression: touching, embracing, intercourse, and the love and affection that one can feel from another. But they have to look at the other side of it and ask, "Can my child responsibly manage this?" It seems to me that many parents get thrown into a tailspin at this time. They may have survived reasonably well with their child for the first twelve years, but now the dilemma is even more aggravated for the most loving families.

If there has been love demonstrated between father and mother, and caring expressed toward children, the child has flourished with that. He has grown to a certain point because of this love and he wants that love to continue. All of a sudden parents realize that they cannot continue to provide it. Parental love does not suffice for a teenager or emerging adult. Love of and from others is needed. Where are parents going to turn now? What is going to happen? This is a very despairing time for many parents. It is extremely frightening. It is often complicated for the family because puberty may occur when the parents themselves are in a transition in terms of their own age and their own interests which extend beyond the family.

Sara: I hear you saying that when the child reaches puberty, his parents are put into an ambivalent situation. On the one hand, all these years they have wanted normalcy for their child and pushed for that in all areas, at home and at school; they have wanted their child to be normal and he may be very normal in his sexual development. On the other hand, now they are pulling back and almost hoping that maybe he is not sexually normal because he is going to place a whole range of problems on his family, with regard to masturbating in public, acting out sexual behaviors, or achieving menstrual care. It seems to me that now the family is in a real guilt bind. Do they want normalcy for this child or do they almost hope that this child will not be normal in the area of sexual development?

Martha: The situation gets more complicated if the adolescent begins to develop a sexual relationship. The partner is likely to come from the special school or actvity center the handicapped adolescent has been attending. Now the family must recognize that their son, or daughter, is bringing *another* person who is less than the expected dream into the family circle. That is shattering to parents; it's as though the world has caved in. You can see the irony of the situation. The more attending, caring, and loving the family has been, the more the young person knows that his feelings are acceptable and the more he wants to perpetuate those feelings and seek love for himself. It's a vulnerable time because he can no longer receive physical attention from his parents or siblings. If he seeks out a seventeen-year-old like his lovely sister, he may be rebuffed. He doesn't understand why. His family has to help this young person deal with the rejections he feels, and they have to accept his relations with his handicapped peers.

At this point in time, many families may need professional help in meeting the varied needs of a handicapped adolescent. Counseling is available through local mental health centers, Planned Parenthood, and religious centers such as Catholic Family Services. Personal hygiene training and medical needs may be met by counseling with the child's physician or a visiting public health nurse. [See Appendix A for a more complete listing of resources.]

But, adolescence is not the end either, because there is, I think, another time when a family is in great stress. That is when the child does not leave the family nest. You see, most children grow up and go away and they establish their own world, their own life space, their own situation. That's what we expect and dream for our children. We expect to be active parents for about twenty years. We are going to have a lovely little boy or girl who is going to grow up and find his own way in the world, and we will be moving toward those free years where we can be less burdened and can anticipate the grandparenting years. Parents of a child with a severe disability requiring ongoing custodial care, monitoring, or support systems realize that their responsibility toward this child is not going to end, but that he will continue to depend upon them for the rest of their lives. This recognition comes at a time when many parents are beginning to feel vulnerable anyway. Many parents begin to experience some loss of health, security, or relationship during the middle years. That's a usual occurrence for middle-aged people, and their problems become compounded because they have one child who is not going to release them from responsibility. It gets to be a very big worry. Who is going to support this child? Who will pay the bills? Provide him a good home? Supervise his leisure time and his participation in the sheltered workshop or educational class? Who is going to keep him out of trouble, keep him from being misused? The parents find that they need to make long-term arrangements for the disabled child in the event of their deaths. They may become extremely depressed, and old guilt feelings may resurface.

We have been talking about at least four times in a parent's life with a handicapped child when the parent had to deal with the same old feelings. First, when he finds out that the child is a special child; next, when his child requires special school programs; then, when puberty begins; and, later, when his child does not achieve independence as an adult.

Sara: We have talked about parents, how these life cycles affect them, and how they have to reexperience many feelings and attitudes and deal with them. What about siblings of the handicapped child? Do they go through similar stages? How are they able to deal with their handicapped brother or sister?

Martha: I haven't had as rich an experience working with the brothers and sisters of a disabled person as I have working with the parents, so how I answer this question is based less on my observations of siblings, and more on reports about them from the parents. It seems that siblings usually reflect the attitudes—healthy or unhealthy—that are modeled for them by their parents. If the parents are accepting and secure as they rear the disabled child, it is usual that the children in the family will have healthy attitudes. To the extent that the parents feel frightened, fragile, and filled with despair, we often see that reflected in their children. It is usual that when the cuteness gives way to the awkwardness of the ten-year-old or to the insecure behavior of the young teenager, brothers and sisters go through periods of being embarrassed. I'm reminded of one particular family that I worked with for some time, where the brothers and sisters had lovingly cared for the handicapped brother. The young boy was not toilet trained and needed to be assisted; he would go to any brother or sister that was available and tug on their sleeve as his signal that he needed assistance. When these brothers and sisters began to bring dates home, they were embarrassed that this brother was constantly needing their attention.

If there is a tremendous expense maintaining the disabled child in the family, brothers and sisters may become resentful of the financial support that is going to this disabled person, especially if they need some of that support for their own career development. Brothers and sisters begin to wonder and worry what will be expected of them in terms of maintaining and supporting the handicapped sibling, in the event that something happens to their parents. They frequently wonder what the possibilities are that they will have a similar child when they start a family.

Sara: As I talk to families it seems that the issue of grandparents is often brought up, and I wish you would deal with that for a minute. How does having a special grandchild affect grandparents and, in turn, how do their feelings affect the parents?

Martha: It's been my experience that when there is an involved grandparent, it is usually a healthy thing in the family. A caring grandparent will help the son or daughter with the special child. Often this provides some welcome respite that parents desperately need. There have been times when I have worked with a family where the grandparent involvement was a negative thing, but generally it has been positive. It's as though the grandparents are able to give understanding and support to their own children in an active way by providing sitter's services, financial assistance, and bringing a lot of attention to the other children so that the parents are free to spend more time with the disabled child. I have felt that it was the fortunate family who had the involvement of the elderly person. I think if we are able to accomplish normalization, it will depend upon how much we go back to being involved as three-generational families, upon the extent to which we will be able to use our extended families. I've always rejoiced with parents when they tell me about their parents, or their brothers or sisters, who lovingly support them as they raise their handicapped child.

How a grandparent handles the acknowledgement of the diagnosis usually is consistent with the way that that grandparent had handled all other crises for fifty or sixty years. It is a lot easier to maintain unreal expectancies for a child over a period of time if you don't have any experiences living with the particular child. I think it is wise of parents to permit, encourage, and ask for as much assistance from grandparents as they can in the early years, because I expect that many grandparents will offer a great deal of assistance if involved from the beginning. The more reality the grandparent experiences, the better equipped he is to provide emotional support.

Sara: So, you're saying that one of the first systems that parents can use is their immediate family and their extended family, and the sooner they do this, the easier it is going to be for the extended family to accept the handicap and offer support. What are some other kinds of support systems that families can use when they find out that their child is handicapped, or as they need ongoing help for him during school age, puberty, and emerging adulthood?

Martha: I would urge parents to be in touch with other parents who have like concerns. No one can speak with more empathy to a family who has a concern about a Down's syndrome child than another parent with the same concern. It proves to be productive for both parents. If I can help two families get in touch with each other, and develop a mutual support system, I have provided them one of the strongest resources available.

Sara: I find that some parents are hesitant or even embarrassed to seek help. One parent told me, "When I seek out help, its admitting that I'm not able to handle my child." How can professionals deal with this? How do we convince parents that none of us are able to handle our problems and that all of us seek help for our children, be they so-called normal or special children?

Martha: I think there are two statements. One is that we seek help all the time for our other children. I don't presume to think I can teach my child; I send my child to school. I don't presume to provide religious training by myself; I send my child to catechism. I am constantly tapping resources for my normal child. It's no different for my child who is special. I think the other statement is this: every individual in the family has some unique needs, and I seek to meet those needs. I do not think it is a mark of failure to seek help from someone outside the home. I'm no dentist; I can't fill my child's teeth. By the same token, if I have a child with a speech problem, I arrange to have my child seen by a speech therapist. We should help people realize that it's an act of dignity to recognize that he may need help from a particular person. We must match all of our children to the services which meet their needs. As a thoughtful parent, I find the best resource I can, and I use it with pride and without apology.

Sara: I think as professionals we often make parents feel guilty for shopping for services. Is shopping for services sometimes a healthy way of dealing with guilt, or coping with having a handicapped child?

Martha: I think that parents get a great deal of comfort from knowing that they are doing the best they can. If there's any question in their minds that perhaps in their community the best is not available, I respect them when they say, "I'm going to check this out." A general practitioner, an educator, or a clinician in a guidance clinic may not be able to pick up all of the intricacies of a concern. I have high regard for parents who go looking for an accurate statement about their child. The thing that is worrisome about that, of course, is the parent who is constantly seeking a miracle—I will run here; I will run there; I will try this; I will try that—as a way of reversing a reality. My hope for parents is that professionals will dare to be honest with them. You see, we professionals have to take some responsibility for parents who shop around, for we are not always honest. Often professionals feel so sorry for the family and the child that they give guarded, or obscure, diagnostic statements. They avoid sharing the developmental potential of the child with his parents. They feel that it is too cruel, too destructive. I challenge that. I think that in most instances a straight, honest statement of what is real is what parents need to hear and we, as professionals, need to help them deal with the grief that comes with hearing the truth. Then we should provide a process over time to help them handle their needs. I think that we now know enough about many disabilities to predict what the future will be. I think we owe it to parents to say to them, "Based on our knowledge now, this is what is predictable about your child." That's hard to do; but to take that position speaks to the integrity and the maturity of the parents and treats them as though they are capable of dealing honestly with the situation. I suggest that for us to do less is a message to the parents that they can't whack it; can't deal with it. If I say there is a message they cannot deal with, I am setting them up to fail. If I treat them as mature adults and say to them, "It is difficult; it is a disappointment; it is despairing; but, the facts are. . . ," then I believe I set up a situation where movement towards healthy management can take place.

Sara: You're not saying, though, that there aren't different degrees of acceptance on the part of the parents, or that parents are not at different developmental levels of their own? How much do you tell a parent at one given time? For instance, when a child is born with a visible handicap, do you then tell the family about what is generally known about the prognosis for the specific handicap; or what he will look like or be like when he is an adult?

Martha: No, but I think the parent needs to hear that this baby who was born today is easily identified as having a handicap and that it is an irreversible condition. I think the person informing the parents needs to be prepared to give truthful responses to any questions that are asked. For example, if a father were to ask me, "Will my Down's syndrome child grow up and be able to walk?" I would say, "In most cases, yes." If he were to say to me, "Will my child grow up and be able to support himself?" I would say, "At this point we are unable to predict that far into the future. He may be able to support himself, or he may need supervision in a sheltered working environment." I think the therapist needs to be attuned to the reaction from the parents regarding each statement. In the best of circumstances we hope that there will be an ongoing relationship between the informing person and the family. Unfortunately, I think that what usually happens is that a medical person makes a pronouncement and leaves the room. He does not stay to deal with the family. I think the best way to handle information is to have the informing person share the truthful statements with the parents together or as quickly as possible with each parent separately. Parents have questions about their handicapped child's life just as they will have questions about their other children; at every stage there are new demands on all parents. Hopefully, there will always be someone with whom they can discuss their concerns. It is important for us to introduce every newly identified family to another family who has recently had a handicapped child. This experienced family will be in a position to offer guidance and support in coping with the problems of having a handicapped child and in seeking appropriate resources. Such a pairing provides opportunities for mutual support as the two families encounter and deal with their similar problems. To work through the grief toward acceptance and management of the family is a heavy, frightening experience.

In society, we all have to deal with death and dying. The whole society is prepared to help its members with that. Think back to any death you might have had in your own family, and you will recall that there was a whole process that got started immediately. The extended family, the neighborhood, and the community reached out and engulfed the family that was in mourning, giving them all kinds of nuture while they dealt with the mourning process. Now, because the birth of a child with an impairment is a less frequent occurrence, society is unable to reach out to the family. About the best society can do is to lovingly, patronizingly, accommodate this newborn child while the child is "cute."

Parents need empathy and support from others who *really* understand and will take the time necessary to work through their feelings of disappointment, fear, and guilt. Such support has not generally been available from the physician, classroom teacher, clergyman, or counselor. As professionals, we must assume responsibility for moving parents of newly identified children with disabilities toward relationships with other parents in like circumstances. The results of such a relationship are mutually productive. The parent who receives the help is comforted; the parent who gives the help is strengthened.

Sara: It seems that you are saying it's the parents who must teach one another how to offer support and assistance. The parents are also the ones who are going to change society, so that society begins to see impaired children as children. Parents are not hiding their children in closets anymore. These children are becoming visible in our community.

Martha: That's what the normalization principle is all about. It's unfortunate, but true, that those of us who have a particular problem always have the additional burden of educating the rest of the community to accept that problem. We see this historically in terms of alcoholism, epilepsy, tuberculosis, and cancer. It is the people who have passed through an experience who can do the best job of helping the rest of us become sensitized. It is also true that families who have a person with a disability must bravely and insistently take that family member into the community so that the rest of us can learn. It will be a more wonderful world when that happens. Look at what we can learn when the handicapped child is mainstreamed into society. We can learn compassion. We can learn to be truly understanding and can begin to accept that the whole human experience is possible for each one of us. I may not have a disability now. One error in driving my car for one block can put me in a handicapping condition. People need to get in touch with that. Your disability is my disability; my strength is your strength. We need to get used to that.

Suzanne Haskin

A New Child Is Born among the Immortals

Our daughter Erin was born on one of the first sunny spring days of the year. Her birth was eagerly awaited as a joyful event by our whole family and followed a normal pregnancy and natural birth. Unfortunately, she was one of the three in 1000 children born each year in the United States with a serious birth defect called spina bifida. Specifically, our little girl was born with an open spine defect called myelomeningocele. The opening was surgically closed within ten hours, and we hoped and prayed for the best results possible.

We were told soon after her birth about many of the complications involved with spina bifida defects. They included partial paralysis below the opening, lack of bowel and bladder control, and the possibility of kidney problems. Such a defect is also often accompanied by a condition known as hydrocephalus. A child with hydrocephalus lacks the ability to naturally absorb all the fluid produced by the brain and this can result in an enlarged head and brain damage.

It was difficult enough to accept all this, but another common complication appeared ten days after birth—meningitis. Meningitis is an infection of the meninges (the lining of the brain and spinal cord). For several weeks we waited for Erin to fight off this first serious setback. She appeared to recover well, and we were allowed to take her home for the first time when she was five weeks old. Within a week, Erin was hospitalized again. Her head had begun to grow—a clear indication of hydrocephalus. The next five months included several more hospital stays for a variety of complicated tests. It was determined that she needed the placement of a shunt device to drain the fluid and relieve the pressure on the brain. However, the placement of the shunt was complicated by brain damage. In time, the doctors were able to implant a double-barreled Holter valve shunt. Erin recovered quickly, and we began looking forward to the future.

Unfortunately, shunts do not always work without problems. The first malfunction occurred three months later. Within twenty-four hours she underwent emergency surgery to clear a clogged valve. Things went very well, and Erin again bounced back quickly. We hoped this would take care of our medical problems for a while. Six weeks later, a more serious problem developed, and the entire shunt system had to be replaced; however, the operation was not successful. For two weeks her condition grew more serious every day until a threat to her life forced another operation. This time the pressure was successfully relieved, but Erin did not recover quickly. In fact, it eventually became apparent that more serious brain damage had occurred. My husband and I had to objectively admit that Erin had regressed markedly and now appeared to be seriously visually impaired, if not blind. Such conditions are hard for any parent to accept, and I believe it takes the passage of time before they can be accepted. We were also confronted with the real possibility that more shunt problems could continue and that Erin's brain damage was progressive. Eventually, the terminal nature of her condition became clear.

After realistically assessing our situation, at least intellectually, we had nearly a year without any serious medical setbacks. During this time, we did our best to see that Erin was happy, contented, and loved. In time, several periods of illness indicated that the head pressure was again increasing. Suddenly, Erin's condition deteriorated and within a few hours she was quietly gone. Her death was so peaceful and dignified that, although our family was deeply grieved, we were grateful that our child had been released from more pain and suffering.

My husband and I have chosen to discuss our daughter's life and death, now, in the hope that we can somehow help the parents of other handicapped children. There are obviously many problems such parents must face. I felt one of the most difficult was that of simply accepting my child's problems. Few of us are prepared before birth for a "special" child. Time and knowledge were the keys to accepting Erin's disabilities for me. Gaining a clear understanding of the specific birth defect with which our child was born gave me the ability to see what she needed, not only in the way of medical care, but also the special therapy needed to help her reach the fullest potential possible. Parents should press physicians and therapists for information regarding a child's condition, even though this may be difficult emotionally.

I feel parents have to face their child's problems realistically before they actively seek all the possible services available to help the child. This is an ongoing problem which isn't just confronted and left behind. Further complications, or just the growth of the child present new situations to accept. Certainly each different type of disability or mental retardation has its own difficult periods. Parents of a severely impaired child must face the limitations of their child's development and the resulting effect on their lives. Parents with mildly impaired children will have problems fitting them into the mainstream of the world, because they are slightly different. Although I stress the importance of objectively evaluating a child's problems and potential, I would certainly also underline that this be done with hope and optimism. Miracles have been performed by hard work and positive expectations.

Financial strains are often placed on a family with a handicapped child, although various agencies are available to make sure medical and therapeutic necessities are covered. A special child often changes the family's financial priorities. This, in turn, usually has some effect on the family dynamics and the separate lives of all the family members. Although the special needs of a handicapped child are very important, I feel it's equally important to be aware of the needs of everyone in the family.

Soon after our daughter's birth, my husband and I seriously discussed the importance of each individual in our family. We agreed that, in the long term, the best way to provide for our special child was for our family to live as much as possible as though she were a normal baby. Decisions regarding Erin which would affect us all were made on the basis of the family unit. In my experience, siblings readily accept and love a handicapped child when the parents naturally do so themselves and when they include the child as an equal member in the family unit. The siblings can share in the good times and the difficult periods. I feel that being as honest and open as possible about the handicapped child's potential and problems is psychologically best for the sibling. The amount and kind of information given should, of course, be judged in light of the sibling's age and understanding level. We began by explaining first about Erin's general condition and obvious handicaps, such as her paralysis. As time passed, our son was gradually informed of Erin's other disabilities. A knowledge of the special child's needs gives the siblings a sound basis for accepting the extra time or attention such a child may require. At the same time, parents must be aware that siblings need attention, and should plan daily periods with them.

In a similar manner, we, as parents of handicapped children, must consider our spouse's needs. Strains in marital relationships are common between parents of a handicapped child. Obviously, each parent is under special pressures. Sometimes it is difficult for us to view objectively the causes of this stress when we are so deeply involved. Parents can be the greatest source of support for one another if they maintain a positive relationship. I think it is very important for parents to make time to be together and communicate. It is also important for both parents to have some time to relax and enjoy their personal interests. I sincerely believe maintaining one's own mental and physical health is one of the best things a parent can do for his children—special and normal.

After reaching some point of acceptance of our handicapped child's difficulties, we next had to determine how to best cope with them on a day-to-day basis. At first, we felt frustrated because there seemed little we could do that was constructive, except see that our little girl had the best physical care and medical services we could find. The amount of support provided by medical professionals varies considerably. Fortunately, we came in contact with several doctors who were quite knowledgeable regarding our child's specific disability. They were sincerely concerned about both our child and our family. Their help was to be invaluable in the difficult times ahead. They helped us set up the routines necessary to take care of our daughter's medical needs.

Being able to feel we had provided the best medical care for our child eased our minds greatly, but being able to work toward constructively helping our child's progress was of equal importance. I personally felt that the early intervention programs in which we became involved provided a great service, not only for Erin, but also for myself. I could not live each day thinking it might bring the inevitable; those thoughts were pushed to the back of my mind while I lived as routinely as possible, working toward small gains in Erin's progress and enjoying her company.

As I look back, the development of normal living patterns in such situations seems important to me. Generally, one cannot undergo the stress of conditions such as a terminal illness without being emotionally drained. Such a high emotional pitch cannot be sustained for very long periods. So, as in our case where there was a negative prognosis, with no idea of the length of the process, I feel it was best to live as normal a life as possible. Programs which brought us in contact with various professionals—speech therapists, physical therapists, occupational therapists, special education teachers, and psychologists—were most helpful. These professionals were qualified to help us set priorities and realistic goals for our daughter's developmental progress. I feel that having constructive activities, aimed at specific goals, helped me normalize my life and prevent periods of depression. The exercises and activities suggested by the therapists were active ways we could participate in our child's development.

In many cases, early intervention programs are very instrumental in making the best use of a special child's abilities. This early, concentrated effort can mean a real difference in the eventual progress made by a physically handicapped or mentally retarded child. The average parent cannot be expected to know the specialized skills which may help his child, but with the aid of the professional, parents can and do learn to be effective treatment givers for their own children.

In our case, nevertheless, there came a time when we realized we must face the real possibilities the future held for our little girl. Fortunately, her prognosis is not a common one, and most parents can look forward to longer and more positive futures with their handicapped children. We, however, were told that Erin's brain damage was quite extensive and that the nature of her problems forecasted future regression and finally death. As time passed, we had to realize that several of her setbacks had resulted in further brain damage and were devastating to her progress. After serious thought, we evaluated the advisability of further medical procedures in the light of their possible effects on Erin's quality of life. Today's medical advances make it possible to continue breathing when all other positive signs of life are gone. We decided to make our little girl's life as pleasant and full of love as we could, and leave the decisions of life and death to God. She was always made comfortable and any pain was eased, but during the last year of her life no extreme surgical measures were taken. Each parent must be guided on this issue by his own understanding of life and his basic spiritual beliefs. We never wanted Erin to suffer in any way, and so, toward the end, we lived with the faith that she would progress until, at some point, she was released from the hindrances of this world.

We were, I believe, justified in that belief. She was only ill a few days before her death and was at home, surrounded by love and all the people and things familiar to her. Her death came quickly and quietly.

Coping with the death of any loved one is difficult, but the death of one's child seems to be even more difficult, because it is not in the natural scheme of life. Of course, we were intellectually aware that eventually we would have to face Erin's death, but emotionally we were never prepared. Only the parent of a handicapped child can understand the deep love I had for Erin, even though she could never respond the way a normal child does.

Erin's death brought drastic changes in the lives of each of our family members. Although we had not centered our lives around her, she was an integral part of our family unit, and her absence left a void which can never be filled. I think several things helped us as a family to work through this experience. First in importance was the love and support, not only of each other, but of our extended families and friends as well. It truly is comforting to be surrounded by those who not only care for you, but sincerely cared for your child, also.

I found my own spiritual beliefs to be important in coping with Erin's death. A personal faith can give you the ability to see the positive aspects of such an experience. We feel that we all grew in many ways because of Erin's life and could never see it as meaningless. Even in her death, we could find positive factors. She died in dignity and peace and did not have to regress to the point of being kept alive artificially, in pain and suffering.

I have found the following quotation from Benjamin Franklin both consoling and inspirational: "A man is not completely born until he is dead. Why then should we grieve that a new child is born among the immortals?"

For a time after our daughter's passing, the most difficult thing for me was changing the daily routine of my life which had so greatly involved her. My son could go back to school; my husband could go back to work; but I could not go back to my previous life. At first, I busied myself away from the house when no one else was there. This kept me from lapsing into depression with too many thoughts of the past. Luckily, both my family and friends involved me in various activities. Contrary to what people often assume, talking about Erin seemed to help, and I valued greatly those friends who could share my memories and thoughts about my little girl. As a family, we also shared our feelings, and these discussions, I hope, clarified our son's understanding and acceptance of death.

I began spending some special time with my son and husband and also took time to indulge myself in regular physical exercise and plenty of rest. Death of a loved one is a draining experience, and the body also needs time to adjust after such a traumatic event.

The attempt to make some positive use of our experiences with Erin by helping others has helped me to stabilize my own life and the lives of my husband and son. I have found it helpful to communicate with other parents of handicapped children about both the joys and sorrows related to our little girl. It is my hope that sharing my experience will be helpful to someone else, just as the experiences and advice of others have often sustained me.

As with most wounds, the passage of time is the greatest healer. It takes time to adjust to the physical absence of a loved one, and time to realize that the memories and love will always remain.

Parents Involved

JOAN YOUNG MEYER

One of the Family

I will begin by saying that our severely retarded son is now eighteen years old. When I was asked to organize my thoughts and even give helpful ideas to other parents as a result of our experience, I knew it was going to be a difficult job. Let me tell you right away that the things that are easiest to remember are the good things. I suspect that may be the most valuable contribution I have to make. One must peel back layer after layer of time to uncover old problems replaced by new ones, some solved and others merely tolerated until they disappear, or we change in order to cope with them. Even these problems have lost much of their sting by the light of a new day, and, I suspect, some of their truth.

To understand how we dealt with our special problems, it is important to take a look at our family situation. My husband and I were both thirty-two at the time Bruce was born. He was the third of four boys. My husband had an interesting job which provided stimulation for him. I had completed my education and had worked before we were married, so I was content with my role of wife and mother. Another important circumstance was that at the time of Bruce's birth, my husband was being transferred to a new community. We had already purchased property in the country. If events could be tailor-made to handle unusual responsibilities, then probably we had most of what was necessary.

The one element which we missed was having our parents close enough to give continuing support and comfort (and baby-sitting) which seem to be the exclusive domain of grandparents. Therefore, from the time our second son was born, I began having a mature woman babysit during the day once a week. We also left the children with her while my husband and I took brief, rarely long, vacations. I learned to go without feeling guilty, and this was to be a valuable asset later when we took trips without Bruce.

The pregnancy was uneventful, but delivery was not. After a short, easy labor the third stage began with the cord presenting itself. The obstetrician was summoned and a fast trip to the delivery room was made. Our baby was born with the cord wrapped around his neck. He experienced early breathing difficulty and was not brought to me to hold for some twenty-four hours. In an examination by a pediatrician before we went home, Bruce was announced to be in good shape.

The "good shape" lasted only a week before we discovered an inguinal hernia. At three weeks, Bruce had the first of two operations for repair of a double hernia. He experienced almost total anoxia as a result of an unexpected reaction to preoperative sedation. The first attempt to operate was abandoned after twenty minutes, during which time he was not breathing sufficiently for the ether to take effect. Forty-eight hours later, the repair of one side was accomplished with difficulty; the second repair was made when he was three months old.

My reason for including the early medical details is that I am unaware of any other early clues which might have predicted Bruce's slow development. The evidence mounted, however, and despite regular visits to the pediatrician, nothing was said. Finally, when he was about nine months old, I was forced to ask the question that almost needed no answer. We were sent to a specialist who said we would have to wait until Bruce was two years old for a diagnosis. As I think back now, I don't think anyone told us anything we didn't already know, and perhaps, as was their explanation, who could do anything anyway?

At the time the final diagnosis was given—brain damage, cause unknown—we were told we should put Bruce in an institution. After a visit to the institution, we took a long, agonizing look at the future for our child. Our decision was to keep him at home, but formally admit him to the institution through the court. This was supposed to allow us to admit him immediately should something happen to us, or should the situation at home become too difficult. As I look back now, those early years were the most difficult of all the eighteen years.

From the beginning, we felt that Bruce should be included in normal household activity. The playpen and baby seat were placed so that he could see and hear what was going on about him. At eight months, when he could use a high chair, he joined us at the table. At about a year, he abandoned the playpen in favor of a roll-chair—a canvas seat suspended from a metal frame attached to small wheels. He became quite skilled in maneuvering this chair, but I can't help wondering if he would have crawled without it. He likewise spent a great deal of time in a canvas jump-chair. As his legs grew stronger, we had to brace the platform so that he wouldn't fall over.

During these early years, we had a regular night-tyrant on our hands. A vacation to visit the grandparents prompted me to request some medication to help Bruce sleep. A mild sedative, given at bedtime for two weeks, was all it took to change what appeared to have been simply a bad habit. It seems strange, now, that it took me so long to seek help, but stranger still that it was not provided before I had to ask.

At about two years of age, Bruce could take a few steps alone, but he seemed to prefer the security of his chairs and a recently acquired small trampoline. This was designed with a bow handle so that a small child could hold on to it while exercising. To this day he uses extraordinary caution in negotiating stairs, descending hills, and in crossing footbridges. He has never had a serious fall, no stitches or broken bones, despite the fact that he rides a bicycle. (We used a tandem to help him gain his balance and self-confidence.)

The only toys which were truly meaningful to Bruce all made music, in one form or another. The stuffed animals with music boxes began the parade. These were eventually followed by boxes with handles and, finally, with knobs. Bruce learned to crank and turn, pull and beat, and do whatever was required to hear the sound. Later, when he could reach the piano bench, he began his artistry which continues to give him so much pleasure today. His playing was never the usual loud, disorganized dissonance. Rather, he has had a style and repetition of phrases which suggest a memory, as well as a dedication to pleasing sound. I have tried to teach him some simple songs, but he resists outside interference.

The record player has been a source of much pleasure for Bruce. He eventually learned to handle it with care. He has been suspicious of new records, often rejecting them for an old favorite. When at last he did see *The Sound of Music* he sang throughout the score, much to the dismay of the audience, probably not matching my own.

Bruce has had a continuing love affair with water. Bathtimes, with all the children, were favorite times. It was, first of all, a time I set aside to give my undivided attention to each child. Second, with no clothes, no restrictions, and the marvelous chance to splash it became Bruce's favorite, as well. It is an easy step from the bath to an outdoor pool, and from there to the lake. We went through these steps with Bruce. However, his lack of fear made him especially vulnerable. It seemed urgent that he learn to swim as quickly as possible, for swimming was a family sport almost daily during the summer. We began by teaching Bruce to use a styrofoam kickboard. Eventually, he was able to use it with efficiency so that he could follow us everywhere. Late the following summer, when he was eight, we forgot the board one day. We were astonished to see Bruce start across the lake by himself. He is an excellent swimmer if, by definition, you can eliminate style and speed.

Our life in the country probably contributed significantly to our ability to cope with Bruce. The pressures of space, close neighbors, traffic, and other children were, by and large, eliminated. The necessity to reclaim our land provided a unique opportunity for father and sons to work together. The work was, in itself, a recreation program which included Bruce. Early in his life he was merely an observer, but later he was able to contribute as well. He still delights in mowing the lawn, but, I hasten to add, not on cue.

As Bruce became more mobile and developed a passion for motors, our vigil had to be increased. During one brief, summer period he put water in the gas tanks of two lawnmowers, water in the underground oil tank, turned off the furnace pilot light, disconnected the water softener, and felled a sizable tree with a handsaw! While these occurred one on top of the other, it was still easier than when he ran away. He started leaving our yard, which had natural boundaries, when he was four. He would simply disappear into the bushes and be gone. Much of the land around our property was uncultivated but covered with large bushes and high grasses. Bruce didn't answer to his name, nor would he come when called. Finally, in desperation, we built a large, fenced area, which included most of the exercise equipment. However, the main exercise then became tugging at the gate. Even for a retarded child a fence can be a put down.

At about this time we were given a year-old German shepherd. The dog became a tolerant companion of all the boys, but especially of Bruce. He seemed to sense that he was to stay with him. From that time on, when Bruce disappeared the dog was close behind, so that when we called for Bruce, the dog came and provided the direction. We also put a hook-and-eye lock on the outside of Bruce's bedroom door, following a particularly frightening experience of finding Bruce's bed empty one night. After a harrowing half hour we found him in a neighbor's garage. Even the dog missed that one!

When he was five, Bruce was enrolled in the school for mentally handicapped children. The school was for trainable retarded children, and it was necessary that they be toilet trained before admission. I accepted the challenge with a daylong vigil, every day for about a week. By the end of that time I was exhausted, and Bruce was no closer to being trained. I decided to wait until warm weather and, with Bruce outside much of the time, I was able to remove all his clothes. I felt if he could see, as well as feel, the results of his performance, we would be farther ahead. By the end of the summer, and with a maximum of two hours a day on my part (I purposely limited the time) he was ready for school.

The school was a half hour away by car from our house, and there were no buses. Since we had a year-old baby at this time, the most I could manage was two mornings a week. It was obvious almost from the beginning that Bruce was in over his head. Nothing in his life had prepared him to sit and color, draw, cut, or paste. He lacked the fine motor coordination, and his interest in everything else made him an unfit subject. It was, nevertheless, a shock when they announced in the spring that they could no longer have Bruce in the school. In any case, we didn't have to wait too long before we learned of a new program being developed with state funds and administered through the local Child Guidance Center. Their classes were held in a church, and there were finally funds for buses. The purpose of the Day Training Center was to provide a program for youngsters who were severely mentally and/or physically handicapped, thereby encouraging parents to keep these children in the community, rather than institutionalizing them. It was tailor-made for Bruce. We are deeply grateful to the concept of the center and to the staff, which somehow managed to put into motion the goals of self-care. It provided us with an alternative to an institution.

The years from six to twelve passed rather easily. We accepted the limitations imposed by Bruce perhaps more easily, because we were immersed in raising our other children as well. We were grateful for good friends. We sought advice from other parents in handling Bruce. The early years with the local Association for Retarded Children put us in contact with parents and professionals who added substantially to our knowledge, and the Day Training Center Parent Teacher Organization kept us abreast of progress at school.

We were aware of the importance that each child should have his share of our time and resources. It concerned me that the temptation to be caught up in the problems of one child should prevent me from obligations to my husband and the other children. I became an extremely efficient housekeeper. Meetings were cut to a minimum and regrets delivered without apology. Many social obligations went unmet, the planning and execution of which left me cross and exhausted. During these years we took trips with our two older boys, leaving the little ones at home. I have regrets now that we didn't do more of this, since our boys remember them in glowing detail. Later we took vacations with the three boys, again leaving Bruce with a sitter, who by now was more like a beloved member of the family than a paid employee. Bruce became accustomed to saying good-bye with a smile, and inevitably, when we returned, we saw that he was calmer and had learned some new skills.

From the age of twelve, things changed rather quickly. I was surprised at the prompt onset of puberty. I had assumed that a child so mentally slow would also be slow in physical development. Wrong! Also at this time, the lives and attitudes of our older boys became more demanding of our attention. The problems of wheels, social needs, colleges, and girls needed our attention and discussion, so the boys could formulate their plan of attack. Work and sports activities needed planning and input from the parents, and while this time does pass, every parent can identify with our need to be available.

Coincidentally, the subtle change of having a retarded child to having a retarded teenager was difficult to manage. I made a feeble attempt to discuss Bruce's sexual development with the pediatrician, but he seemed more embarrassed than I, and suggested that I not borrow trouble. At the time, local newspapers were carrying summaries of professional meetings concerning the need to protect retarded adults from compulsory sterilization. Few medical and other professional people seemed interested in the impact which sexuality has on the entire family of a retarded person. We feel there are times when, upon informed parental consent, sterilization may be necessary for a person who cannot assume responsibility for his actions, and we continue to be aware of various situations which may be difficult for Bruce to manage.

Also during Bruce's teenaged years, we consulted an attorney about a will. The only question we had was how long Bruce could be expected to live. We have never asked that question, but we deal with each day as it comes. We sought legal counsel from another source and did complete a will tailored to Bruce's and our family's special needs.

Many attorneys are unable to advise families of the handicapped on legal issues because of an ignorance of the scope of handicapping conditions, or because they do not see the rights of the retarded in the perspective of the whole family. (I think if there had been a panic button to hit, these were the days I would have!) When planning for the future of their retarded child, a family should choose a lawyer who has some knowledge of handicapping conditions and the rights and life care needs of the disabled, as well as an empathy for the needs and rights of the family. Any will or trust fund provisions should be general enough to cover any uncertain events, yet meet needs specific to that handicapped individual and his family.

By the age of fifteen, Bruce's abilities and character were well established. He was healthy, happy, and well-adjusted. His speech was almost nonexistent, despite therapy at school and much effort at home. He obeyed simple commands, not always without a growl. His days which had been full of activity were now spent increasingly just sitting in a chair, so that school became even more important to his well-being.

The terminal illness of my mother and threatening health problems of my own brought the developing situation quickly to a head. We requested that Bruce be given respite care in the institution. This was denied, the institution explaining that they had one respite care bed for five counties. A request was then made for placement in a group home for teenagers in a nearby community. Eleven months later Bruce was admitted.

Bruce's adjustment to the home was immediate and enthusiastic. The first visit home was a huge success, and my worries that he wouldn't want to return were unsubstantiated. Over the years, Bruce had gone away to camp. I believe this past experience helped him to accept his new home and seven "brothers and sisters" more easily. We see Bruce often. He attends the same school and most of the youngsters living in the home are classmates. We feel this is the best of all possible arrangements which could have been made. We are grateful for the skill and perception of the social worker from the institution who helped us make the change.

Rather than project plans for Bruce's future, it seems more useful to put in a word or two about his family. The mother of any child must be prepared to make necessary adjustments in her life, both before and after the birth of her child. A portion of that responsibility can be shared, but, at least among our contemporaries, it is still the woman who bears the lion's share.

During Bruce's early years I was happy to be at home. I would have been very grateful for any therapeutic help when he was an infant, but there was none available at that time. I was able, from my readings, to provide stimulation for him throughout the day, but I was eager for professional help. By the time Bruce was five or six, I was ready to again enter the professional world. It had never occurred to me that eventually I would not be able to return to my profession. As the family grew up, however, I realized that it would be impossible for an employer to accept my special restrictions.

When Bruce was finally accepted into a program, I was grateful that the Day Training Center did not encourage parental involvement in other than typical school functions. I had spent twenty-four hours a day for six years with my child and this freedom (even though it was only twenty-five hours a week) allowed me to volunteer for positions in social and health agencies in the community. This relief from constant child management allowed me the luxury of contributing and increased my own feelings of worth.

Our three other boys have contributed much to our ability in handling Bruce. They suggested guidelines for our role as parents and prevented our indulging in pity for Bruce or ourselves. Who else would have thought to buy a used chain saw, guaranteed not to start, for a delighted, retarded brother for Christmas? The boys never complained that the conflict of Bruce's bus schedule kept them from participating in after-school activities and sports. They babysat with Bruce until the youngest was heard to exclaim, "I bet I'm the only guy in town who babysits his older brother." I am glad for their sakes that a genetic study shows that they have no more chance of having a retarded child than the population at large.

And the father of this family? Well, he has been a marvelous father. You could set your watch by his arrival home each day. Somehow he managed to leave the problems and frustrations encountered in his work at work. He worked daily with the boys outside, summer and winter, teaching them to cut and split wood, gardening, all about the differences in his beloved trees, skiing, sledding, skating, hiking, canoeing, and on and on. Inside, he taught them chess, workings of the business world by having them chart stocks, and shared his talents for fixing almost anything. As the boys grew older, he maintained a formidable profile not to be challenged. I hinted that, as mother, I had the major responsibility, but only until father came home. Then the problems and difficult decisions could be shared.

SARA L. BROWN

A Structure for Early Parent Involvement

The Philosophical Framework

The philosophical framework of this chapter evolved from the experience gained in working with parents through the Early Intervention Project for Handicapped Infants and Young Children. The philosophy is based on nine premises which present parents as capable, caring people. These premises offer a basis for a service delivery system which is efficient and effective. The philosophy offers a solid foundation for any handicapped child/parent intervention system, but it is especially applicable for children who function under the developmental age of three.

Parents are concerned. When professionals involve parents in programming for their handicapped children, they must first believe that parents have a genuine concern for the welfare and development of their child. This premise is the foundation of any parent involvement model, for every other feature is built on it. Parents generally do care for their child's growth and want to maximize their child's development. There are degrees of care and commitment, but, with help, all parents can become actively involved in the treatment of their child on a daily basis.

Parents are effective treatment givers. During the attachment period (birth to three), parents are the most effective treatment givers. Professionals who can spend only a few hours a week with a child cannot hope to have the influence over the child's development that a parent has on an hourly basis. Research on early attachment of the child points to primary caregivers as critical to the child's learning process. The child grows from an egocentric stage, where *he* is the world, to a point where his parents become the most important influence in his world. Much of what he learns will be due to the opportunities and stimulation which they provide. To expect professionals to substitute for the parents in the development of a young child is unrealistic.

The environment is important.   The home is a young child's classroom and playground combined. Normal children learn to walk, talk, play, investigate, and achieve independence in their home environment. An early intervention model which utilizes the home environment allows natural learning to occur through play and routine care and handling activities.

Parents need skills.   Few parents enter parenthood with the necessary skills for promoting their children's growth and for developing good interaction patterns with their children. Parents of handicapped children need additional parenting skills and special therapeutic skills for maximizing their child's development over time, while still maintaining a normal family life.

Skills promote competency.   When parents gain skills in parenting and therapeutic techniques, they begin to have successes with their child. Parents who learn handling techniques to enhance a cerebral palsied child's movement begin to experience success when they feel a change in muscle tone. Parents who demonstrate skills in play activities with their child see positive changes in that child and begin to feel a part of those changes. Successful experiences lead to feelings of competency and worth.

Competency yields positive interaction.   Feelings of confidence and competency are reflected in parent's daily interactions with their child. Parents who have a taste of success develop a desire to achieve even more changes in their handicapped child. Competency leads to increased positive social interactions between parent and child. Generally, both verbal and nonverbal communication behaviors increase with parental feelings of success. The stage is set for the ping-pong effect between parent and child (Gordon, 1975). A parent who feels good about his parenting looks at, touches, smiles at, and talks to his child. The child responds. The parent imitates the child's response. The child repeats and the communication cycle is completed.

Parents need support. Professionals can be helpful by encouraging parents to express and work through feelings of anger, frustration, and guilt concerning their handicapped child. However, a professional cannot fill the role of another parent. Parents who share mutual problems, feelings, and successes in raising handicapped children are best equipped to support and counsel other parents in the areas of daily handling and caring for their child.

Parents are members of the team. Parents come to professionals at various levels of development, just as their children do. (For a more complete discussion of this concept, see Meister, 1977.) Some have already gained skills in handling and treating their child; others have not yet worked through their feelings of rejection and fear. Some parents are initially committed to involve themselves in their child's program; others need encouragement. Some parents have excellent communication with their child; others have developed few interactions. All parents can be trained, in a variety of ways and at various commitment levels, to become competent members of the treatment team; although educational, socioeconomic, and employment status of the parent sometimes determine his level of commitment. The professional must be sensitive to the coping mechanisms and to the tolerance level of each individual parent. In some families, the primary care giver may be a grandparent or older sibling. Continued contact with the family in both the group and home visit sessions helps the professional to individualize the training program to meet the parents' level of commitment, as well as the child's needs.

Parents are advocates. In most states, the services offered to the handicapped child are due largely to the efforts of organized parent groups. Professionals working with parents must be able to help parents learn of their legislated rights, anticipate future unlegislated needs, and advocate for their child's medical, educational, vocational, and avocational needs and living standards.

Three Features of an Effective Early Intervention Model

An effective model consists of three major aspects: treatment, training, and support. Since these three features overlap extensively, the goals for each can be met within the above philosophical framework. In order to provide the best treatment for young children, the focus of the program should be directed toward their parents. If parents are to be trained to become primary treatment givers, planners, and advocates for their children, necessary avenues of support must be developed.

The Treatment Model

Early intervention services can be delivered through home and group-based treatment sessions, formal and informal evaluations, and therapeutic programming. Because of the therapeutic needs of involved children, on-line staff should include a speech and language therapist, a physical therapist, and an occupational therapist. As well as being responsible for the treatment sessions, the therapists can share the responsibility for comprehensive evaluations on a consistent basis with the psychologist. The special educator can offer his services in preschool testing, by serving as a liaison with school districts, and by developing behavioral management programs. Individualized, assesment-based programming in the six areas of development (gross motor, fine motor, cognition, social/ emotional, language, and self-care) increases treatment accountability. Programming for children in areas of strength, as well as weakness, helps assure success for the child and further develops possible compensatory skills.

Children with all types of handicapping conditions (mental, emotional, motoric, and sensory) can be integrated into group-based sessions. Developmental level should be the major factor in determining groupings. Although initially referrals may primarily include mildly involved preschool children, many of these children can soon be mainstreamed into public schools and private play or educational settings. As time passes, and early intervention programs gain publicity and credibility in the community, the children referred will be younger and more severely involved.

As programs evolve, there may be major changes which will direct the focus of the staff to parental training as a primary goal. First, as they work together, the staff will begin sharing skills. As new skills are gained, role changes may begin to occur, until each staff member feels competent in offering some counseling, teaching, and skills in the other disciplinary areas. This interdisciplinary growth is a necessary part of a parent training model. A staff member cannot expect a parent to learn skills in all areas when he lacks these skills. The home visitor must develop his skills to include a number of interdisciplinary techniques if he is to be successful in monitoring the child's treatment services and providing parental training. Severely involved children often may have medical complications which prevent group attendance. The home visitor is more effective when he has a variety of skills and has been trained to know when his skills have been exhausted and he must call in a fellow professional to help.

The Training Model

Parents can be encouraged to participate in every aspect of their child's program, as indicated on the flow chart. They must have some initial commitment to become involved in their child's treatment, but can then become the final decision makers regarding major programming plans for their child.

Many early intervention referrals may be self-referrals. Parents learn of programs through medical and educational professionals, visiting nurses, or friends. For reasons of confidentiality, a professional should not act on a referral until the parents are informed that a referral is being made.

The initial contact with the family may be by telephone. A staff member may call the parents, asking them to express their concerns about the child and requesting a home visit appointment. Most parents called will be eager to have a staff member visit in their home. If the family does not have a phone, a joint home visit can be made with a staff member of the referring agency, with the parents' consent.

The initial home visit can serve as an excellent source of information about the family, give some indications as to how the parents perceive their child's needs, and offer the home visitor a chance to informally screen the child. It also allows for a description of the program and an opportunity for a staff member to invite the parents to visit a group session before making their final commitment.

When parents visit a group session, they have the opportunity to talk with staff members and ask questions of the other parents present. It is an opportunity to see what their responsibilities will be as parents in the program, as well as to see the services in action.

If the parents decide to enter the program, an evaluation can then be mutually arranged. Evaluation can be done in the home for medically involved or at-risk children under doctor's orders to re-

Flow Chart of Early Intervention Project Parent Training Model

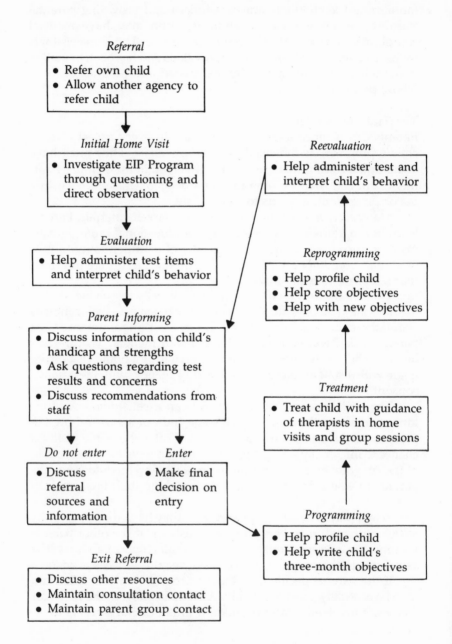

Referral
- Refer own child
- Allow another agency to refer child

Initial Home Visit
- Investigate EIP Program through questioning and direct observation

Evaluation
- Help administer test items and interpret child's behavior

Parent Informing
- Discuss information on child's handicap and strengths
- Ask questions regarding test results and concerns
- Discuss recommendations from staff

Do not enter
- Discuss referral sources and information

Enter
- Make final decision on entry

Exit Referral
- Discuss other resources
- Maintain consultation contact
- Maintain parent group contact

Reevaluation
- Help administer test and interpret child's behavior

Reprogramming
- Help profile child
- Help score objectives
- Help with new objectives

Treatment
- Treat child with guidance of therapists in home visits and group sessions

Programming
- Help profile child
- Help write child's three-month objectives

main at home. Otherwise, both parents should be present during their child's evaluation in the clinical or educational setting. A parent informing session can be held a week or so after the evaluation. This is an excellent time to train parents to discuss their child's behavior and to begin to understand the stages of child development. The session also offers them the opportunity to ask questions regarding their child's strengths and weaknesses.

The parents should be encouraged to bring their children to the group while their interest and commitment to the program are acute. Home visits should also begin as soon as possible on a regular basis. Both home and clinical or educational settings can serve as sites to train parents as members of the treatment team.

When parental priorities are recognized and included in program objectives written every few months, parents are encouraged to become more involved. Parents can participate in the formal evaluations which take place periodically (suggested time is every six months). When the program's resources for a given family or child are exhausted, or a major programming change is necessary, a parent informing session should be held to prepare parents for future problems and to help them seek out new resources. The child should be placed in another service setting whenever possible. Settings may include local and intermediate school programs, private schools, nursery or day care settings, or programs offered by service organizations such as United Cerebral Palsy. The exit process should occur over time to ease the child's transition and to prepare the parent for autonomy and advocacy.

The Supportive Model
The supportive aspect of an early intervention model can be interwoven throughout treatment and training activities. Continued professional support should be given to the families through listening, counseling, suggesting, and seeking resources. When the family meets a medical crisis, the home visitor can aid that family by spending extra time with them at the hospital or clinic. When respite care is needed, the staff can assist the family in finding such care. When financial burdens become too great, appropriate resource services can be contacted. When additional therapeutic counseling is needed, the family should be referred to a community mental health center or another agency.

Professional support is an important facet of any program working with families, but parent-to-parent support is even more valuable. As parents become more competent and relaxed with their own child, as they work through feelings and solve problems, they begin to share their coping and problem-solving skills with newer parents. Perceptive mothers can be especially helpful in integrating new mothers into the program and supporting them by phone. Fathers can be helpful by openly discussing their child's problems and their own fears without embarrassment. Monthly parent meetings can offer formal programs on area resources, normal growth and development, and discipline; as the group evolves, discussions of feelings and coping techniques can be held. Less formal, but just as effective, contacts can be made at the weekly group treatment sessions, where parents can share everything from recipes to football scores.

Coordination of an Effective Intervention Model

The interweaving of the features of treatment, training, and support is highly dependent upon an effective coordinator. Staff members can rotate, so that they all serve as coordinators of the services rendered to families through their program and other contributing agencies. It is the coordinator's responsibility to see that services are not duplicated, or that one does not contradict the other, and that communication channels between agencies and staff within those agencies remain open and used. The case coordinator is ultimately responsible for keeping complete records on the family and for anticipating potential problems before they occur.

In some cases, the case coordinator may feel that it is necessary to ask another staff member to share a case with him. Severe medical or emotional problems of a family and child may be so draining on the coordinator that he is unable to effectively continue his work with that family. In other cases, the coordinator may feel that he has lost his objectivity after working with a family over a period of time.

The case coordinator serves foremost as supporter of the family. He knows the family best because of frequent contact with them, generally serving as their home visitor. He understands their circumstances, their child's needs, and can best support them during times of medical, emotional, or financial crisis.

The case coordinator is the natural spokesman or advocate for the family. During the weekly staff meetings, he informs other staff members as to the immediate needs of the child and family and "defends" them when he feels others do not understand the family's coping tolerance. Within the community, the case coordinator attempts to encourage professionals in other agencies to understand why a family responds in a particular way to services provided. One who visits a home on a weekly basis is probably best able to interpret family responses, which evolve from the family's own complex set of dynamics and problems. The case coordinator can also serve as advocate for the child and family at educational and medical placement meetings.

The case coordinator is, finally, a resource seeker for the family. Depending on the ability of family members to seek and use resources, the case coordinator seeks help appropriate to that family; he is interested in that family as a complex unit, not just as parents or siblings of the handicapped child. A father might be aided to seek vocational training. A mother, who wants to finish her high school degree, can be referred to appropriate educational services. Another mother might be referred to a resource which can help her search for a new home. Case coordinators soon learn that financial, medical, and emotional crises often occur in families; the treatment of the handicapped child must be put into the perspective of these larger needs.

Summary

For services to be rendered effectively using the model described in this chapter, professionals should recognize their additional responsibility as advocates and advocate trainers. The child will receive the most appropriate services and the parents will receive the most effective training and support when professionals begin to speak on the behalf of handicapped children and their families and to train parents to accept their advocacy role.

One of the best illustrations of the role of the advocate is seen in multi-agency parent-informing sessions. The early intervention case coordinator can accompany parents to these sessions with doctors, public health nurses, other educational professionals, and/or community mental health personnel to: (1) advocate for the child's programming needs and strengths based on his professional expertise and knowledge of the child, and (2) model for the parents acceptable ways of gaining information and expressing priorities for their child.

By modeling problem-solving communication in these ways, the coordinator can narrow the gulf between parents and the professional world.

REFERENCES

Gordon, I. 1975. *The Infant Experience* (Columbus, Ohio: Charles E. Merrill, Inc.).

Meister, S. 1977. "Charting a Family's Developmental Status—For Intervention and for the Record," *The American Journal of Maternal Child Nursing* 2:43–48.

GAY S. MCDONALD

Parents' Home Ground

Each individual entering a new role brings with him a set of skills and competencies that enable him to function and feel confident in that role. The level of skills and competencies varies with each person. The parental role is no exception.

In preparation for the parental role, a skill and competency base is acquired and refined over time. There will have been opportunities to model and imitate parenting behaviors of one's own parents and friends. If the parenting role is not a new one and there are other children in the home, a parent has the advantage of drawing on his past experience with earlier born children. However, the individual placed in the role of parenting a handicapped child usually finds that his acquired skills and competencies are not sufficient. An appropriate interactional base for dealing with and handling the child effectively is lost. Parents of handicapped children need to be taught specific skills and proficiencies for the daily handling, care giving, and, in some instances, playing with their special needs children. Parental confidence needs to be restored so as to promote the appropriate interaction with the child.

It is believed that all parents have the desire and ability to develop additional skills and competencies in the handling of their children, and that the home is the primary learning environment for the young handicapped child. With accessibility to the child twenty-four hours a day, the parent is in the best position to give therapy on an ongoing basis. Professionals who see the child only two to four hours a week necessarily have limited involvement. The parent also has the advantage of having a longitudinal experience with the child and is in a better position to compare past and present functioning. Most important, the child remains with the parent for life. The parent must be taught new skills and competencies to enable him to interact confidently, consistently, and comfortably with his handicapped child.

The nature of parental involvement in an early intervention program must be carefully planned. Home visitation is an obvious and effective opportunity for fostering the active involvement of parents.

Involvement in a Natural Setting
In order to include family involvement as a planned, purposeful part of a program dealing with young handicapped children, professionals must know the families with which they interact. The basic routines of daily living within the home, current interaction patterns among family members, and the alternatives available for both the family and the environment must all be known before planning the program. Such information helps the professional to plan an effective treatment program—one that will generate family support. Professionals cannot expect parents to carry out prescribed treatment programs which fail to consider the parents' skills and competencies or the environments in which they must function.

Initial Visitation
It is often helpful if the first contact with the family following the referral is a home visit. In this initial contact, a representative of the staff explains the types of services which can be provided and the expectations which will be placed on the family (home visits, attendance at group sessions, etc.). The initial visit serves as an opportunity to assess the knowledge of the parent regarding the child's handicap, demands placed on the parent by other family members, and the environmental limitations. A short informal assessment of the functional level of the child may be carried out at this time.

A Move Beyond the Mother
The mother is not the only member of the handicapped child's family. Through the home visit component, professionals can expand the role of care-giver beyond the mother, if this is compatible with the family's life-style. The goal is to involve as many family

members as possible in the care-giving and stimulating roles. By increasing the number of family members who interact with the child, the family achieves integration of the child into the family unit, allowing attitudes and roles to become more normalized.

The nature of involvement may not be the same for all family members. Each member can participate in ways which reflect his own special interests and skills. The goal is to make the child/family interaction pleasant and relaxed.

Siblings are great at devising simple games to build imitation skills and promote cognitive development with the handicapped child. Modified games of peekaboo and hide-and-seek can be used to reinforce auditory localization skills and the concept of object permanence. Such games also promote locomotion. Fathers can be encouraged to assume some of the basic care of the child. Bath time may be reserved for the father and may prove to be positive and enjoyable for both the father and the child. When other family members are involved with the handicapped child, the mother has an opportunity to spend time on herself or with other family members. The handicapped child also benefits from such an arrangement. He gains the opportunity to experience other interactional styles and to develop feelings of independence and autonomy.

Routines
Within an early intervention program, the home visit may focus on the establishment of routines for the treatment of the handicapped child by family members. For this reason, therapies for the child are devised to fit within the usual patterns of family interaction. Bathing is one good time for carrying out needed therapies. If a child requires range of motion exercises, the soaping and rinsing of limbs provide an easy way to achieve the needed movement while the child is relaxed. Balance is also promoted. Water play (pouring, splashing, toy dunking) provides good reinforcement for the concept of gravity and cause and effect relationships. Bath time also allows ample opportunity to work on imitation skills and vocalizations.

Staff members can work toward the goal of helping the family to feel comfortable and confident in the handling and care of their handicapped child, to assume the same type of responsibility with their handicapped child as they do with their nonhandicapped children.

Time for Sharing
The home visit is not only a time for the training of specific therapy techniques, but also a time for the sharing of specific problems that the family is experiencing in rearing their handicapped child. Parents are often more willing to express their problems in the comfort of their home than in a clinical setting. As relationships grow between the home visitor and the family, there will also be an increased sharing of some of the concerns and fears for the future of the handicapped child. The necessity for the future provision of care for their handicapped child is often the biggest concern of parents. Parents may be interested in the composition of wills, facilities where respite care might be obtained, and possibilities for institutional care. Home visits become a time when parents can ask questions privately and, hopefully, get answers related to their personal needs.

Additional Support
Although the term *home visitation* is used, visits may not be limited to the home. In a model which emphasizes total treatment for the child, the program staff must follow the child. If the child spends his day in a day-care center or with a day-care mother, he may be visited there, and help may be provided to the individuals working with him to integrate routines and therapeutic activites into his schedule. When the child becomes ill and requires hospitalization, the program staff may visit him at the hospital and continue to give support to the family. If the family is seeking help for the child from another agency, it may be appropriate for the home visitor to accompany the family.

Summary
Effective parental involvement in any early intervention program is a result of careful planning. The home visitation component provides the staff an overview of the skills and competencies of the parents and the types of limitations placed upon that family. Coupled with the specific therapeutic needs of the child, this information allows for the establishment of a treatment program which the family can support on an ongoing basis.

As a staff, the professionals should strive to make the parents an integral part of the intervention team. Parents should be welcomed, needed members of any therapeutic team providing services to their handicapped child, and the successful intervention staff will convey this confidence to parents throughout its program.

LINDA R. GRASS

Families Together

Introduction

There are two types of groups which play essential roles in an early intervention program. One type is designed for parents and their children; staff members use these groups to model and instruct parents in treatment and management techniques. The second type is usually designed for parents only. Its purpose is to support them in their parenting roles. These groups can be held in any convenient location; in sparsely settled rural areas, they may be held in parents' homes on a rotating basis. At these treatment sessions, the staff, parents, and children have opportunities to gain support, expertise, and a variety of practical ideas from one another. Often it is easy for the handicapped child and his care-givers to become isolated from other children and adults, resulting in the loss of feedback from external realities that others in the community can offer. In group sessions this potential difficulty is averted. In fact, participation in group activities often becomes the springboard for more participation in the family's community.

Oftentimes, parents are not able to meet their child's special needs because of a lack of social support, difficulties in working with a variety of professionals, or a lack of knowledge and skills related to their child's handicap. With the help of professionals and other parents in the group, parents of handicapped children can become empathetic, knowledgeable treatment givers while maximizing their roles as parents. The parents' feelings of helplessness and inadequacy, often crucial roadblocks to family functioning, lessen as knowledge, skill, and acceptance of responsibility increase. The parents begin to play an active, rather than passive, role in their child's growth.

Group Treatment Sessions as a Training Opportunity

Meeting Needs. In working with groups of young handicapped children, there must be a great deal of flexibility in the composition, scheduling, and curriculum of the treatment session as dictated by the changing needs of the children and parents. There should be a purposeful effort to integrate various types of handicaps and ages of children within a group. This variety offers each handicapped child opportunities to model higher functioning children; it offers the parents the chance to view their child's areas of strength and weakness. It also gives them a realistic picture of their child as compared with different types of children.

When children have a special need for language or oral stimulation, extra sessions may be scheduled. These sessions allow the parents to observe staff and other parent models and to develop skills in speech and language training.

Although the majority of care-givers attending the group sessions will probably be mothers, a number of fathers may be able to come, either on a regular or intermittent basis as their work situation allows. Fathers may come when they are unemployed, work late night shifts, or rotate with their wives who work. If their jobs prohibit attendance, a father's group might be considered. Some fathers may be reluctant to work with their child when they do not have direct contact with the child's program. A night or Saturday morning father's group could be an option, serving a number of purposes. Fathers might appreciate a monthly group session where they could bring their child to the school or clinic without their wives. This would give them opportunities to learn techniques and skills directly from their child's teachers and therapists. More traditional work groups could be formed to improve the treatment facility or grounds, or to plan and construct play equipment. Such groups could be planned to appeal to fathers' interests, talents, and schedules in a mutually supportive setting.

In some cases, the grandparent may be the primary care-giver and will become the focus of training. Other parents may bring their neighbors, babysitters, siblings, or relatives to the group sessions. The sessions can also serve as excellent means of coordinating agency services to the child; public health nurses, day care or nursery teachers, and other therapists can attend.

Mothers who work may be able to arrange their schedules so that they can attend some weekly sessions. A single parent having an 8:00 to 5:00 job may wish to take vacation time once a month to come in with her child.

Strategies for Training. Group sessions offer both direct and indirect training opportunities to parents and staff. These adults demonstrate and model attitudes and techniques for working with disabled youngsters, teaching and learning from one another. In addition to feeling less isolated and inadequate in dealing with their children, parents will be able to develop friendships and to pool needed information, such as where to obtain the services of a capable baby-sitter, how to respond to relatives' questions, where to go for transportation services, etc. Unstructured times can be planned for social exchange, observation, or relaxation. These can be balanced by structured times, when the parents actively participate in the treatment of their child. The specific objectives devised by both staff and parents for each child can be worked on in the sessions. Activities chosen to meet these objectives should be apporpriate to the developmental level of the child to assure success for both parent and child. The group sessions often allow the parents to use a variety of types of equipment not found in their homes. Parents can also draw on the experience of other parents in adapting activities or toys for their child.

Another effective strategy is to switch children among parents to give them experience in working with children of different abilities and temperaments. Another person is sometimes better at selecting appropriate techniques to achieve the desired response, than is the natural parent.

Problem Areas. In any early intervention program, two of the major problems regarding group session attendance will be transportation and absenteeism.

If the program's funding does not provide for transportation, several alternatives may be explored. Parents who live near each other may be able to car pool. Other parents can use the bus system and may be reimbursed by the Department of Social Services for their fares. Red Cross, Social Services, and other volunteer agencies often provide transportation for families.

Absenteeism in early intervention programs is generally quite high. Although this may be initially discouraging to the staff, it is understandable. Young children have a lot of illnesses; young handicapped children are even more susceptible. In the northern climates, the weather often adds to this problem. Parents do not like to take a chronically ill child or a child susceptible to respiratory problems out in winter. Icy roads contribute to lower group attendance, also. Because of the nature of handicapping conditions, many parents do not feel it is safe for their child to ride in a car when the danger of accidents is increased due to road conditions. The staff may encourage attendance by suggesting ways to dress the child, the use of special seats and seat belt arrangements for car traveling, and by assuring productive learning sessions when the parents do attend.

Siblings of the Handicapped Child

Because of babysitting problems, some mothers may find it necessary to bring siblings to the group sessions at times. If the siblings are of appropriate ages to provide models of normal speech, ambulation, play, and self-help skills, both the handicapped children and the parents can benefit from the children's participation. The siblings will gain a greater understanding of handicapped children through this experience.

If it becomes difficult for a number of parents to get babysitters, a sibling group may be formed. Parents can alternate being in charge of this group in a nearby room. Such a plan allows the parents to interact with normal children. The siblings receive the attention of trained staff and parents. At the same time, staff members can become more familiar with the handicapped child's total family.

If there are a number of siblings above the age of seven or eight, they might benefit from a rap group, planned and led by a professional with some experience in facilitating children's discussions. The sibling rap group puts the children in contact with one another (thus providing them a support system) and gives them an outlet for expressing their frustrations, fears, and anxieties over having a handicapped sibling. The rap sessions can be helpful, however, only when carefully planned and when positive attitudes are fostered.

The professional's job is done when planning sessions, home visits, and the group treatment sessions are completed for the week. For the parent, however, the job is continual, and it is emotionally draining. Social isolation, overwhelming feelings of anger, depression, and helplessness can set in at any time. To become aware that there are others enduring the same problems can help parents cope with these feelings. To meet and discuss issues as a group is even more conducive to mastery of these dilemmas.

There are various organizations presently existing as support groups. These share a common circumstance, stress, condition, or position. Examples include Alcoholics Anonymous, Parents Anonymous (for parents of battered children), Adoptees Anonymous, Single Parents, groups for widows, those who have had mastectomies, and others. The "anonymous" designation interestingly exhibits society's lack of complete acceptance of human variations. It also indicates that there is a certain degree of social isolation that occurs for those involved.

Parents of handicapped children likewise need to identify with "those who have been there." To understand empathetically means not only to acknowledge intellectually, but to experience affectively. This empathy is enhanced when two people have experienced similar stressful conditions and can acknowledge those concomitant feelings. It is often difficult for the parents of a handicapped child to admit to the difficult times and feelings they have. As though others would disapprove or disavow their nonacceptance, anger, grief, exhaustion, wishes, and "unrealistic" hopes, they must keep these feelings inside. Yet, unless one openly admits to human reactions and situations, one cannot cope with and overcome the negative consequences of these bottled up experiences. Those who share their experiences can more easily elicit expression from each other and, most importantly, help one another in solving mutual problems. Sharing the hardships, offering emotional support, assisting with practical advice, and pooling both resources and information can be available for parents through parent groups.

Certain topical issues proposed in a parents' group may involve inviting guest speakers. Information and encouragement to anticipate future schooling, sexuality issues, self-care, vocational training, and group living can be obtained from a reputable source, such as the mother and father of an adolescent handicapped child. Resource speakers from the community can discuss topics such as community sponsored recreation programs for preschool handicapped children, behavioral management of the severely delayed child, alternative educational facilities, the preparation of wills and trusts, institutional placement, and respite care.

Admitting their initial confusion and despair helps parents to share with each other. By talking about past and present hurts, they can offer comfort to one another and the assurance that such feelings are not unique. As the group continues, other issues may be voiced: fear of being rejected by the spouse, other family members, or the community; a neighbor's response to their child; and rearing healthy siblings. They can share various methods for coping and problem solving in the areas of discipline and setting expectations for the severely involved child. Grandparents, extended family members, and other support and advocacy systems can be discussed.

Many parents have feelings of guilt and self-reprehension; in the parent group they not only receive support from other parents, but they can also see how unproductive, although realistic, these feelings are.

The meeting times must be flexibly set so that as many parents as possible can attend, i.e., avoiding night football and Saturday baseball game times if fathers are expected to attend. The meetings may last two to three hours. Babysitting services can be made available through the staff or interested college students.

Potluck suppers may be especially effective in motivating total family participation. At such gatherings, families with similar problems can socialize and see each other in a new dimension. Siblings can meet with and talk to other children who have handicapped brothers or sisters, giving them opportunities to make friends and develop their own support systems.

It is a testimony to the success of a parent group when it continues to meet, even though the children have moved on to a variety of placements throughout the community. From their shared experiences, parents have recognized their special bond and ways in which they can help one another.

Robert M. Segal

The Elderly
Handicapped Person

A Historical Perspective

The care of children has always been a major concern in our country. It is not surprising that in the development of services for disabled persons, priority has been given to the needs of children. Segal (1975) points out that the two major historical events that shaped the development of programs for the disabled in the United States were (1) establishment of parent organizations in the 1950s and (2) passage of the Maternal and Child Health and Mental Retardation Planning Amendments of 1973 (Public Law 88–164).

The focus of program development for disabled persons during the past twenty years has been in the area of children and young adults. Little has developed with regard to the needs of the disabled aged person.

Most research and training efforts in the field of disabilities have focused on children and adolescents with a progressively decreasing focus on the older populations. A search of the literature, regarding programs and services or research in the area of the elderly developmentally disabled, indicates practically nothing has been published (Dickerson et al., 1974).

This focus on services for children continued through the decade of the late sixties and early seventies. Recognition was given to the need to implement programs and services for handicapped infants and children, both in terms of prevention and treatment, as a means of maximizing the potentials of disabled children through interventions in the prenatal, perinatal, and early childhood periods.

A Double Jeopardy

Why has the development of service programs for the developmentally disabled older persons been neglected? Contributing to this neglect was probably the prevailing public opinion that the handicapped person tended to die young, particularly the severely or profoundly handicapped person. Another reason was that there was a lack of advocacy for the older person.

Probably the most salient factor has been that disabled persons were seen as less worthy of the expenditure of funds. Our culture has always placed great value on youth; therefore, to be old is to be a less valued human being. To be old and to be handicapped as well places a double stigma upon an individual, putting him in double jeopardy.

A Broadening Perspective

In recent years, however, attention has been extended to the needs of the adult handicapped person for several reasons. Since the children who were being served by the program of the 1950s have grown older and need programs to meet their changing age levels, programs for older persons are being developed.

Because of advances in medical and health care, for the general population as well as for the handicapped persons, the elderly are living longer. There is a need to plan programs and services for this specific population, and it requires a broader knowledge base for the planner and for the practitioner in the fields of the aging and the handicapped.

A change in attitude was revealed in 1975 when the National Association for Retarded Children, recognizing the need to broaden its focus, changed the word *children* in its title to *citizens*, thus reaffirming that organization's primary objective as stated in its bylaws: ". . . to promote the general welfare of the mentally retarded of all ages, everywhere."

Also, in recent years an emphasis has been placed on examining the needs of the elderly in general and, along with this, the needs of the elderly handicapped, particularly the elderly mentally retarded. For example, Hamilton and Segal (1975) reported that at a recent national conference on Gerontological Aspects of Mental Retardation, efforts were made to highlight the service needs of the elderly retarded and to ascertain the kinds of programs that were being provided to this population.

In 1976, the federal Office of Developmental Disabilities recognized the need to develop training programs for personnel working in the field of developmental disabilities. It funded five projects of national significance which focused on the needs of adult and aged handicapped persons. These projects were to be implemented in Georgia, Michigan, Nebraska, Utah and Oregon.

Much needs to be learned about the problems of the aged handicapped and the solutions to these problems. This paper will attempt to examine some of the problems that elderly disabled persons face and propose suggestions for solutions.

Impediments to Obtaining or Providing Needed Services

Despite the need for programs and the apparent recognition that the disabled (particularly the elderly disabled) need services to improve their current functioning, there are numerous blocks that hinder not only the obtaining of services, but also the development of new services and the utilization of existing ones. The impediments may be described as follows: (1) lack of awareness by consumers of the location or the existence of services; (2) poor distribution of services in various parts of a community or state, i.e., the rural area is often without any services for the developmentally disabled, while the city may have duplications of existing programs; (3) lack of trained professionals to work with the elderly developmentally disabled; (4) problems of accessibility of services for the elderly disabled, i.e., services are often in locations not easily accessible by public transportation; (5) discriminatory zoning which prohibits the utilization of certain geographic areas for the establishment of group homes or other services; (6) negative community attitudes towards developmentally disabled aged persons which affect the availability of housing and/or employment opportunities; (7) lack of funding for the development of needed programs; (8) lack of agency coordination of existing services; (9) lack of community awareness of the problems of the elderly developmentally disabled; (10) difficulties in identifying the elderly developmentally disabled within the community; and (11) absence of services to the elderly developmentally disabled persons in many existing generic services.

Identification or location of the elderly handicapped person is a major problem. Kriger (1974) pointed out that it was extremely difficult to find data of this kind. She felt that this was due to the fact that there was no central reporting mechanism for this type of information in many states. Categories and statistics are often classified in one or two categories, such as children or adults. The adult category is usually considered to be all those individuals who are over the age of twenty-one. Dybwad (1961) pointed out the difficulties of obtaining accurate data on the population of the elderly developmentally disabled. Dickerson, Hamilton, Huber, and Segal (1974) also pointed this out in a paper significantly titled, "The Aged Mentally Retarded: The Invisible Client." Segal (1972) pointed out the difficulties of trying to identify and locate the elderly developmentally disabled person, particularly the mentally retarded person who had been discharged from a state institution and was living in the community.

Studies undertaken by Temple University (1977) and by the Rehabilitation Institute of Chicago (1977) indicate difficulties in identifying elderly handicapped persons. Incidence and prevalence studies need to be implemented to identify the elderly developmentally disabled clients so as to determine their existing needs.

Service Needs of the Aging Handicapped Person

In a recent study undertaken by Northwestern University and the Rehabilitation Institute of Chicago (1977), it was found that the greatest unmet needs of handicapped adults were (1) transportation, (2) vocational training, (3) employment placement, (4) financial aid, (5) residential placement, (6) information and referral services, and (7) education. While these needs were quite apparent in the adult developmentally disabled person, they become even more exaggerated and crucial for the elderly individual with developmental handicaps.

In another study of the medical and allied health services delivery systems for substantially handicapped adults (Temple University Rehabilitation and Training Center, 1977), unmet needs for services in the following areas were reported: (1) physical medicine and rehabilitation, (2) dentistry, (3) speech, (4) psychological diagnosis and evaluation, (5) counseling, (6) transportation, (7) recreational services, (8) day care services, (9) vocational services, and (10) educational services.

Physical Problems Confronting the Aging
Handicapped Person

The elderly handicapped person is often likely to have less stamina and may find himself more easily tired as his bodily functions slow down. This may be a temporary or permanent state and may be related to an existing handicapping condition which may continue to deteriorate as he ages.

Studies have commonly indicated that physically limited persons may have a lowered capacity for flexibility, adaptablility, and dexterity. The lower performance level is often more closely related to the particular disability, rather than just to age, sex, or physical stature. However, when disability combines with the natural aging process, it may very well exacerbate the already existing physical limitations. The aging process also brings a higher incidence of arthritis, diabetes, heart and stroke conditions, and the accompanying ramifications.

Other Problems Faced by the Aging Handicapped
In addition to a lack of needed services, the elderly disabled population encounters social problems related to interaction with others. They are likely to face separation from friends and/or family members due to death, or because of placement in housing which is distant from both relatives and friends.

Another problem that the aged disabled person experiences is the increasing sense of dependency which the aging process brings. This dependency may stem from general handicapping conditions or from declining physical health. Because of inabilities to maintain self-help skills, elderly handicapped persons may feel overwhelmed about their future. They desire protection from life's threats. Hitov (1975) discusses the phenomenon of *transfer-trauma* which occurs when the elderly handicapped person is moved from one place of residence to another. He states that the feelings experienced by many elderly persons as they are moved from one institution or nursing home to another and the emotional shock created by such precipitous changes can, and often does, cause severe depression, regressive behavior, or even the death of the elderly person.

As these elderly persons change their residences or experience the loss of family, relatives, or friends, they may be cast into states of confusion. In being moved from a familiar environment to an unfamiliar one, such a person may experience loss of identity and a sense of isolation , which increases his dependency and reduces his freedom to act.

Sexuality of the Aging Handicapped
Cohn (1973) states that the prevailing view on the part of society is

that geriatric sexuality is not necessarily desirable. This view has often prevented elderly disabled persons from normal sexual functioning.

Often residents of nursing homes or institutions are made to feel that sexuality should not be discussed, and the whole question of sexuality is avoided. These residents, therefore, rarely talk to the staff about their sexual feelings or needs.

For the elderly male disabled person, who may previously have been sexually active, the possibilities of a decrease in sexuality are quite real; this is seen in the general population as well. We must recognize the continuing meaningfulness of sexuality for the elderly disabled person and provide counseling and opportunities for sexual expression and fulfillment for this group.

Maintaining Intellectual Capacity and Potential for Growth
Mc Leish (1976) points out that the aging process itself should not indicate that the mind necessarily deteriorates. For example, at age seventy-one Tolstoy completed the novel, *Resurrection*, writing all of its 200,000 words by longhand. Voltaire wrote his classic *Candide* at age sixty-four. Will Durant, in collaboration with wife, began to write five volumes of the *History of Civilization* at age sixty-nine; he completed the study at age eighty-nine.

Retirement, then, may not necessarily mean a dead end. The aging process leads to less effective functioning, but it "can unleash the creative drive pent up for years." While reference has been made to the more normal elderly person, professionals must recognize that in the handicapped person, the aging process may also unleash the creative drive. Senility may not be a consequence of aging but rather a false label imposed by society.

The Need for Spiritual Support
A major contribution to the elderly disabled person's feelings of worth, dignity, and meaningfulness may be achieved through continued religious education or through religious affiliation and church activities.

One of the most potentially important community resources for the elderly disabled person is the church, which serves as a vital component in the structure of the community. It is imperative that the church, which is beginning to provide programs for the disabled child and young adult, become more involved in serving elderly handicapped persons. Some church groups are already providing residential care, counseling services, and opportunities to participate in worship services to the elderly disabled person. Those who have attended church services while in institutions, nursing homes, and communities often state that religion has a great deal of meaning for them. The religious experience continues to have meaning for them and they look forward to church services or visits from the clergy.

The elderly disabled person's continuing adjustment to the community is often difficult. The hospitality and the spiritual support offered by the church can go a long way toward making the aged person feel that he belongs. One elderly handicapped woman stated that it gave her a great deal of pleasure to attend church services each week. She felt accepted by the people in the church, and that feeling of acceptance was very special to her.

As the disabled person grows older, he shares feelings similar to those of normal individuals; he wonders about death, especially after he has lost parents or friends. As his life draws to a close, the need for a religious experience and the desire to get closer to God may increase. Too often professionals working with the disabled person think primarily in terms of the physical, educational, vocational, or social needs of the handicapped person. They often overlook the important spiritual needs of the disabled elderly person. This need becomes increasingly important as the religiously inclined person approaches the end and begins to review his past life. He questions the meaning of his remaining life and the meaning of life after death. He may need help with this quest.

Solution I: Planning Programs for the Elderly Disabled in Institutions

Many institutions are notorious for the poor quality of residential care they provide for disabled persons. While this notoriety is often justifiable, it has created additional problems. In the foreseeable future, there may be some residents—particularly elderly handicapped persons—for whom an institution may be the only appropriate residence. Personnel will be needed to work with these residents. It is extremely demoralizing to relatives of the disabled person deciding to institutionalize their family member to hear only destructive criticism regarding institutional care.

It is important that those responsible for institutional activities explain attempts to improve programming. Words like *warehouse* do force us to examine the dehumanizing aspects of institutional care, but they do not tell the whole story. Some institutions and nursing homes are making valiant efforts to provide decent care to the elderly developmentally disabled person. While the institutional system needs to be revamped and undergo drastic change, simply crying for the overthrow of the institutional system is not the answer, at least in the foreseeable future. Fortunately, there are forces at work that are trying to restructure the total institutional system to determine how that system can provide more appropriate care. While we may not be able to abandon institutions entirely, we can restructure and redesign them so that the needs of the adult and elderly disabled residents will be met. We must attempt to do the following: (1) restrict residential populations to numbers for which facilities are designed; (2) utilize the setting more productively as an outpatient facility, developing greater ties to the community; (3) increase salary levels and provide financial incentives so as to upgrade the quality of staff; (4) implement more in-service staff training for personnel at all levels; (5) upgrade specifically needed programs for the multiply handicapped, such as speech and physical therapy programs, (6) develop closer working relationships with relatives of the residents; (7) improve the inadequate physical aspects of the facility; (8) provide improved socialization programs that more meaningfullly prepare the resident for return to the community; (9) develop the mechanism for adequate compensation for work assignments within the institution; and (10) develop a positive image of the institution by providing rehabilitative, rather than simply custodial, care.

If institutions utilize these models and implement rehabilitation programs, cries to tear down the institutions may be modified. The real question is not whether there should or should not be institutions, but whether, as a society, we care enough about the welfare of disabled persons to provide them with high quality programs based on humanitarian concerns.

Solution II: Community Placement Programs for the Elderly Disabled

More and more frequently the elderly developmentally disabled are remaining in the community. They are either transferred from state institutions to community-based nursing homes or to private group homes. Some may be able to live with their families. There is a need for the expansion of existing community services if elderly disabled people are to function more effectively within the community.

Some of the following program changes that will improve

community-based services are: (1) more family involvement, from the preplacement phase through the follow-up process; (2) better preplanning and counseling with the resident regarding his release from the institution; (3) improved institutional programs to realistically prepare the resident for release so that his behavior will be more appropriate to community living; (4) better coordination among agencies, such as mental health and social services; (5) clearer and more realistic administrative procedures that will facilitate program planning for the resident; (6) an improved monitoring system that will examine the merits of community placement homes and community-based programs; (7) improved clarification regarding legal jurisdictional responsibility for the resident once he is placed in the community; (8) expansion of existing community programs and development of new programs to assure such needed services as financial assistance, counseling, vocational training, recreation, health care, and all of the other supportive services that will help handicapped persons to become as independent as possible; (9) an adequate and more realistic approach toward funding nursing home care programs in the community, so as to upgrade the quality of skilled care in these residential facilities; and (10) an expanded community educational program to effect positive changes in the community's attitude toward the elderly disabled client.

Solution III: Parents, Siblings, Professionals, and Volunteer Organizations As Advocates

Parents, siblings, and other family members of elderly disabled people have basic responsibilities to advocate on behalf of the handicapped person. The issue of consumer rights is as pertinent to the rights of elderly persons as it is for any other population. Consumer organizations, such as the associations for retarded children, cerebral palsy, and others all have histories of advocacy and of serving as "watchdogs" to ensure the adequacy of programs on all levels. Now, with the more recent development and expansion of community placement programs, the need for these organizations to step up their watch dog role is urgent. Consumers and consumer representatives, whenever they recognize an inadequacy in services, should contact their legislative representative, the Department of Mental Health, or the Department of Social Services, whichever is responsible for institutional or community-based programs. Voluntary organizations, such as Citizens for Better Care

(Detroit, Michigan), have played the advocate role and have served as watchdogs in calling to the attention of the community and the press any violations of human rights found in nursing home services. Often the volunteer organizations and representatives of the handicapped have utilized the court system to defend the human rights of disabled persons. This demand for changes in the service delivery system should continue until the system more adequately meets the needs of the elderly population.

In addition, professionals must monitor the quality of care in community programs. They must speak out against injustices and violations of the legal and human rights of disabled persons wherever they are seen, whether in the institution or in the community. Both professionals and paraprofessionals must develop effective mechanisms within the system itself to safeguard the adequacy of programs, without endangering the welfare of the client and without damaging the program.

Solution IV: Ongoing Research
More research needs to be undertaken regarding the needs of the elderly disabled person. Dickerson, et al. (1974) indicate that the following questions warrant further study:

1. Do disabled persons tend to age more rapidly than the normal population? It was noted that many disabled individuals tend to become prematurely old. There seems to be a noticeable physical deterioration in their health condition (i.e., high blood pressure, dental problems, etc.). Is this premature aging process directly related to the factors of their disability (i.e., chromosomal disorders) or is it due to poor medical and health care?

2. To what degree is the aging process of disabled persons more pronounced because they have not learned self-care skills or because severe limits have been placed on their educational and training opportunities?

3. Do aged disabled persons residing in state institutions live longer than the aged disabled persons residing in the community?

4. Do some house parents in group homes and some nursing home personnel tend to infantilize disabled persons? What is the basis for this behavior and what are the best methods to alter it?

5. How can disabled persons be identified once they have been discharged from state institutions? For example, when they are placed in nursing homes, their record may not be sent and the staff often is unaware of their backgrounds or specific needs. What kinds of organizational procedures need to be devised to help the community agencies be more aware of the special needs and backgrounds of this population?

6. Why have so few surveys been undertaken to identify the aged disabled person in the community? Agencies serving the handicapped seem interested in identifying children or adults so as to develop programs for them, but they do not seem as interested in the aged disabled.

7. Why has so little thought been given to preparing the adult disabled person for his old age? There may be a need to develop programs in state institutions and in community group homes that prepare the adult disabled person to handle the problems that may arise during the aging process.

8. Is it true that many handicapped persons seem to bypass the middle-age phase? That they move from childhood to prolonged adolescence and then into old age? Is this related to their disability, or to the way they were handled or programmed by society and the environment in which they live?

9. To what degree are disabled, aged persons different from normal, aged persons? Some agency personnel feel that their problems are similar and that no special concern or attention is required. This view has serious implications for the development of specialized programs, especially for aged retarded persons.

Summary
Historically, services for disabled persons have focused primarily on the needs of children. In recent years, attention has been extended to the adult and elderly. However, negative professional and community attitudes toward the elderly disabled person have tended to block program development.

The elderly handicapped person is confronted with many obstacles to his social adustment, both within the institutional setting and within the community. Before programs can be implemented to help resolve these social problems, it will be necessary to identify the elderly people and to make assessments of their needs. Then the available community resources can be evaluated in terms of meeting such needs.

There are numerous impediments to providing needed services to elderly disabled persons. Such obstacles as lack of information about existing services and lack of knowledge on how to make appropriate referrals preclude many from getting the services they need. Furthermore, lack of trained personnel and of community awareness regarding the plight of the elderly person prohibits the effective utilization of existing services.

Studies have indicated that the greatest service needs of the elderly disabled person focus in the following areas: (1) transportation, (2) vocational training, (3) financial aid, (4) residential placement, and (5) medical and allied health services. In order to implement and develop these services, additional funding and improved community interagency coordination will be needed.

Because disabled people now have longer life expectancies, it is imperative that programs and services be implemented to meet the pressing health, social, economic, and housing needs that confront them as they grow older. More information is needed about this special population, which previously has been regarded as the "invisible client." More research needs to be undertaken in this area. Most important of all is the need to emphasize the continuing capacities of elderly handicapped persons for growth and productivity.

REFERENCES

Cohn, S. 1973. "Geriatric Sexuality: An Overview and a Survey." Unpublished paper, Ann Arbor, Michigan.

Dickerson, M.; Hamilton, H.; Huber, R.; and Segal, R. 1974. "The Aged Mentally Retarded: The Invisible Client—A Challenge to the Community." Paper read at the Annual Meeting of AAMD, Toronto.

Dybwad, G. 1962. "Administrative and Legislative Problems in the Care of the Adult and Aged Mental Retardate," *American Journal of Mental Deficiency* 66: 716022.

Hamilton, J., and Segal, R., eds. 1975. *Proceedings of a Consultation —Conference on the Gerontological Aspects of Mental Retardation* (Ann Arbor: University of Michigan).

Hitov, S. 1975. "Transfer Trauma: Its Impact on the Elderly," *Clearinghouse Review* April.

Kriger, S. 1975. "On Aging and Mental Retardation," *Proceedings of a Consultation—Conference on the Gerontological Aspects of Mental Retardation*, edited by Hamilton, J., and Segal, R. (Ann Arbor: University of Michigan), pp. 20–32.

McLeish, J. 1976. *The Ulyssean Adult: Creativity in the Middle and Later Years* (New York: McGraw-Hill).

Northwestern University, Rehabilitation Institute of Chicago. 1977. "A *Study of the Medical and Allied Health Services Delivery System for Substantially Handicapped Developmentally Disabled Adults* (Washington, D.C.: U.S. Department of Health, Education, and Welfare).

Segal, R. 1972. "The Community Placement Program—A Challenge to the Community, the Institution, the Resident, and the Family." Paper read at the Third Annual Spring Conference, Institute for the Study of Mental Retardation, Ann Arbor, Michigan.

_____. 1975. "The Aged Mentally Retarded: A Challenge to the Church," *Journal of the National Apostolate for the Mentally Retarded* 5: 16–17.

_____. 1977. "Trends in Services for the Aged Mentally Retarded," *Mental Retardation* April.

Temple University Rehabilitation and Training Center. 1977. *A Study of the Medical and Allied Health Services Delivery System for Substantially Handicapped Developmentally Disabled Adults* (Washington, D.C.: Department of Health, Education, and Welfare).

Appendices

Resources for Families

Editor's Note

Early in the life of your handicapped child, you should be aware of the many resources from which you can secure help for a variety of needs. As the child becomes older, needs change and you again must seek resources. This search continues throughout the life of the child.

Specific resource listings vary from state to state. *Appendix A* is a listing of general types of resources to be found in most cities or states. Some will appear in the local telephone directory. If a specific item cannot be located, contact another resource in the same group. For example, if you wish to investigate genetic counseling, the Public Health Department, March of Dimes, private physicians, or Planned Parenthood could provide information on such counseling in the local area.

Appendix B is a listing of national organizations related to professional disciplines and to specific disability areas. Correct names and addresses are listed. Large organizations usually arrange for mail to be forwarded if addresses are changed. Small and recently formed organizations sometimes list the private home of an officer or director as the address. These are more difficult to trace in the case of changes. Consider calling the desk of the local library for help in locating agencies. If there is a college nearby, call the department which seems most closely associated with the disability area, such as the special education department for help in locating a group concerned with learning disabilities or Down's syndrome. Hospitals or schools can be contacted for locating professional organizations, as these agencies include members of many professional organizations. Do not expect the telephone operator to provide the information. If you are seeking information on the American Occupational Therapy Association, call a local hospital and ask to speak to an occupational therapist. Answers to questions related to handicapped persons can be obtained by writing *Closer Look* (see p. 156). New organizations form as needs arise. Ask teachers, nurses, physicians, and other parents if they know of any new organization in your area of concern.

Appendix C lists and gives short descriptions of major laws which provide protection and services to handicapped persons. You should become familiar with these rights in your continued search to provide the best for your child.

Appendix D is a bibliography which lists books of interest and gives a brief description of each title.

Appendix A

General Resources

Education
1. Local school districts
2. Intermediate school districts
3. Private schools, day care centers
4. Adult education programs
5. Information on handicapping conditions (library, parent group, national organizations)
6. Vocational Rehabilitation Service
7. Local universities, colleges, community colleges
8. Local church groups

Financial Help
1. Child and Family Services and other social service agencies
2. Local service clubs (e.g., Kiwanis, Rotary, Civitan, Women's Clubs, Jaycees)
3. Crippled Children, March of Dimes, Medicaid
4. Catholic Social Services
5. Crisis centers
6. Social Security Assistance (federal)
7. Long-term financial planning through trusts, wills

Health and Medical Services
1. Public Health Department — Visiting Nurse Association
2. Private physicians, dentists, specialists, well-baby clinics
3. Specific disciplines (e.g., audiology, nutrition)
4. Mental health clinics, child guidance clinics
5. Crippled Children, March of Dimes, Easter Seal Society, United Cerebral Palsy
6. Planned Parenthood

7. Genetic counseling
8. Cooperative Extension Service (nutritional consultation)
9. Early Periodic Screening Diagnosis and Treatment (available to all Medicaid patients from birth to age twenty-one)
10. Alcoholics Anonymous
11. Drug abuse centers
12. Parents Anonymous

Lifetime Planning and Care
1. National, state, and local organizations (such as Association for Retarded Citizens)
2. Lawyers (trust funds, wills, commitment)
3. State and private residential facilities
4. Nursing care facilities

Recreation and Leisure
1. YMCA-YWCA
2. Drop-in centers
3. Community recreation programs (parks and recreation departments, church groups)
4. Boy and Girl Scouts of America
5. Youth day and summer camps
6. Special Olympics
7. Adult education classes
8. Senior citizens groups

Respite Care
1. Baby-sitters
2. State and regional institutions
3. Foster homes
4. Day care mothers
5. Drop-in day care centers
6. Local advocacy groups (Association for Retarded Citizens, Association for Children with Learning Disabilities)
7. Crisis centers
8. Halfway houses
9. Group homes
10. Salvation Army

Support Services
1. Parent groups
2. National, state, and local organizations which offer advocacy services, such as Association for Retarded Citizens
3. Community mental health, counseling services
4. Child guidance clinics

5. Legal advocacy groups
6. Protective Services
7. Family Resource Center
8. Catholic Social Services
9. Jewish Family Services

Transportation
1. Public transportation (bus, taxi, dial-a-ride)
2. Volunteer drivers, Red Cross, and other service organizations
3. Social Services
4. Local church groups

Vocational Services
1. Vocational Rehabilitation Services
2. Sheltered workshops
3. Goodwill Industries
4. Salvation Army
5. League for the Handicapped
6. Local school districts
7. Intermediate school districts

Appendix B

Professional and Disabilities Organizations

Alexander Bell Association for
the Deaf
3417 Volta Pl., N.W.
Washington, D.C. 20007

American Academy for Mental
Retardation
IIDD
1640 W. Roosevelt Rd.
Chicago, Illinois 60608

American Association for the
Education of the Severely/
Profoundly Handicapped
Box 15287
Seattle, Washington 98115

American Association on Mental
Deficiency
5201 Connecticut Ave., N.W.
Washington, D.C. 20015

American Civil Liberties Union
22 E. 40th St.
New York, New York 10011

American Foundation for the Blind
15 W. 16th St.
New York, New York 10011

American Occupational Therapy
Association, Inc.
6000 Executive Blvd.
Rockville, Maryland 20852

American Physical Therapy
Association
1156 15th St., N.W.
Washington, D.C. 20005

American Speech and Hearing
Association
9030 Old Georgetown Rd.
Washington, D.C. 20014

Architectural and Transportation
Barriers Compliance Board
Director
Washington, D.C. 20201

Bill Wilkerson Hearing and Speech
Center
1114 19th Ave., S.
Nashville, Tennessee 37212

Children's Defense Fund
1520 N. Hampshire Ave., N.W.
Washington, D.C. 20036

Closer Look
Box 1492
Washington, D.C. 20013

Council on Exceptional Children
1920 Association Drive
Reston, Virginia 22091

Crippled Children's Society
2023 W. Ogden Avenue
Chicago, Illinois 60612

Cystic Fibrosis Foundation
3379 Peachtree Rd., N.E.
Atlanta, Georgia 30326

Down's Syndrome Congress
c/o Betty Buczynski
Membership Chairman
16470 Ronnies Drive
Mishawaka, Indiana 46544
(newsletter)

Easter Seal Society for Crippled
   Children and Adults
2023 W. Ogden Avenue
Chicago, Illinois 60612

Epilepsy Foundation of America
1828 L. St., N.W.
Suite 406
Washington, D.C. 20036

First Chance Network
Early Education Program
OE/BEH
ROB 2009
400 Maryland, S.W.
Washington, D.C. 20202

Ina Mend Institute
Human Resources Center
Dept. 33
I.U. Willets Rd.
Albertson, Long Island, New York
   11507

John Tracy Clinic
806 W. Adams Blvd.
Los Angeles, California 90007

March of Dimes
P.O. Box 2000
White Plains, New York 10602

Mental Health Law Project
1751 N Street, N.W.
Washington, D.C. 20036

*Michigan Association for
   Emotionally Disturbed Children
2355 Northwestern Highway
Southfield, Michigan 48075

National Association for Children
   with Learning Disabilities
5225 Grace Street
Pittsburgh, Pennsylvania 15236

National Association for Down's
   Syndrome
170 N. Harvey
Oak Park, Illinois 60302

National Association for Retarded
   Citizens
2709 Ave. E, East
P.O. Box 6109
Arlington, Texas 76011

National Association for the
   Education of Young Children
1834 Connecticut Ave., N.W.
Washington, D.C. 20009

National Center for Law and the
   Handicapped, Inc.
1235 Eddy Street
South Bend, Indiana 46617

National Society for Autistic
   Children
621 Central Ave.
Albany, New York 12206

*At the present time, the state organizations are autonomous.

Office of Child Development
330 Independence Avenue, S.W.
Washington, D.C. 20201

Office for Handicapped Individuals
Department of H.E.W.
Washington, D.C. 20201

President's Committee on Mental
   Retardation
Regional Office Bldg. #3
7th and D Streets, S.W.
Washington, D.C. 20201

Spina Bifida Association of America
343 S. Dearborn
Chicago, Illinois 60604

United Cerebral Palsy
66 E. 34th Street
New York, New York 10016

University Affiliated Center
AAVAP
2033 M Street, N.W.
Suite 406
Washington, D.C., 20036

Appendix C

Major National Laws
Affecting the Handicapped

A Word About the Law

When a law is passed by Congress, it is named, numbered, and filed. Little explanation regarding interpretation, compliance, and enforcement is given, but most laws include a directive to the Office of the Secretary for expansion and interpretation.

The Office of the Secretary reviews the law and the legislative minutes to develop guidelines and procedures which are then published in the *Federal Register*.

Laws are first divided into *Sections*, and *Titles*, and then into smaller units. Since laws are reviewed and amended frequently, the numbers, sections, and titles are changed almost immediately. Therefore, over a period of two or three years, the law itself may undergo major revisions.

Parents can write their state and national congressional representative to obtain the most recent information on a specific law. It is helpful if the name, number, and date of the most recent law or amendment can be given. Contact with congressional representatives is even more important prior to the passage of laws, so that specific concerns regarding services for and rights of handicapped persons can be expressed.

General Laws Affecting Handicapped Persons

1. Education of the Handicapped Amendments (1974), Public Law 93–380, relates to *privacy and confidentiality*. Title VI, Section 612 gives parents the right to examine all records and suggest corrections when needed.
2. Vocational Rehabilitation Act (1973) Public Law 93–112 deals with *civil rights*. Section 504 assures civil rights by prohibiting discrimination of the handicapped in all programs which are federally funded.

3. The 14th Amendment to the Constitution is the law most commonly referred to as a protection of *civil rights* for the handicapped.
4. Developmental Disabilities Assistance and Bill of Rights Act (1975), Public Law 94–103 establishes the *right to treatment, service, and habilitation*. Section 112 requires states to submit a plan of habilitation for the dependent handicapped client. Section 113 requires states to advocate for the dependent handicapped client.
5. Architectural Barriers Act (1968), Public Law 90–480 mandates *free access* to all buildings housing federally funded programs (e.g., ramp substitutions for stairways, accessible doors, etc.). *Access to public buildings* is further defined in the Vocational Rehabilitation Act (1974), Public Law 93–112, Section 502.

Education
Education of All Handicapped Children (1975), Public Law 94–142 provides:
1. Free *educational services* to all handicapped persons from three to twenty-one years of age by 1980.
2. *Educational services* determined for each individual as based on formal evaluations by qualified people within the school district.
3. *Educational services* in the "least restrictive environment" which may lead to mainstreaming.

Employment
Developmentally Disabled Assistance and Bill of Rights Act (1975), Public Law 94–103 provides:
1. *Employment opportunities* through affirmative action by all state agencies or rehabilitation facilities.
2. *Employment opportunities* through affirmative action by any programs under Federal contract.

Institutional Commitment
Developmentally Disabled Assistance and Bill of Rights Act (1975), Public Law 94–103 provides:
1. Public care in the "least restrictive setting" (e.g., to encourage community programs and acceptance of responsibility).
2. Limits placed on involuntary commitment.

Human Research Subjects
National Research Act (1974), Public Law 93–348, Section 202 provides:
1. Requirements for informed consent.
2. Protection of "institutionalized mentally infirm" persons in research programs.

Appendix D

Editors' note: Although there are a number of books on parenting and stimulation now available at the local bookstore, few good books are geared toward the parents of a handicapped child. The following bibliography is a listing and description of the books determined most helpful to these "special" parents because they deal with specific adaptations for the handicapped child or because their material is universal and applies to the rearing and stimulation of all children. The annotations were compiled after an extensive library search by its authors and personal contributions by many authors of this volume. The first section, Child Disabilities, contains books written to instruct parents, teachers, and therapists in rearing and teaching handicapped children with a variety of disabilities. This section is subdivided into general books which are applicable to all types of handicapping conditions and books written for more specific populations such as brain damaged, mentally retarded, cerebral palsied, etc. The other four sections are: Growth and Development, which outlines normal child development; Parenting, which describes parenting styles applicable to all types of children; Play and Stimulation Activities which, although written largely for all children, describes activities adaptable to the handicapped child; and Siblings, which includes books geared toward siblings of the handicapped from preschool to high school age.

NOTE: (PB) designates that the book is available in a paperback edition.

Gay S. McDonald and
Pauline L. Wright

Annotated Bibliography

Child Disabilities

GENERAL

Apgar, Virginia and Beck, Joan. *Is My Baby All Right?* New York: Trident Press, 1973.
A book about children who are born with serious defects and disorders occurring before or at the time of birth. What causes the defect? Could it have been prevented? Is it inherited? Will it happen again to a second child? The book aims to answer these questions. It is written with a nontechnical vocabulary but uses terms the parents of a special child are likely to encounter from the professionals who are helping them.

Ayrault, Evelyn West. *You Can Raise Your Handicapped Child.* New York: G.P. Putnam's Sons, 1964.
While many books deal with what should be done for the handicapped, this volume deals with how to do it. Parental feelings and attitudes are discussed as the major factors determining the effect a given therapy or approach has on the successful handling of the child.

Buscaglia, Leo F. *The Disabled and Their Parents: A Counseling Challenge.* New York: Charles B. Slack, 1975.
Written by the parent of a disabled child, the book stresses the need for counseling support to the disabled and their parents to relieve feelings of frustration, confusion, and fear. It is also intended as a challenge to all professionals who work with the disabled and their families to become more cognizant of the need for good, sound, reality-based guidance, and the tremendous resultant despair and loss of human potential when guidance is not forthcoming. All parents of handicapped children can benefit from this book.

Cohen, Shirley. *Special People.* Englewood Cliffs, N.J.: Prentice-Hall, 1977.
The publisher's description of this easy to read, comprehensive coverage of age ranges and disabilities is, "It offers hope for the parents of disabled children, for teachers, for employers, and most importantly, for the disabled themselves, that with increased information and continuing technological advancements, society will allow the disabled to live fully, independently, and with self-respect." Excellent reading lists dealing with various handicaps and personal accounts of the problems and coping mechanisms of persons of all ages are included.

Foxx, Richard M. and Azrin, Nathan H. *Toilet Training in Less Than a Day.* New York: Simon & Schuster, 1976. (PB)
Based on a toilet training program perfected for adult males in an institutional setting, this book outlines toilet training measures for parents who would like to complete such training quickly and successfully. It requires an intensive commitment on the part of the parent who must toilet and pump liquids through the child consistently and often throughout the training period (which may take longer for a retarded child).

Heisler, Verda. *A Handicapped Child in the Family: A Guide for Parents.* New York: Grune & Stratton, 1972.
The focus of the book is on the psychological adjustment of parents to the special problems of their child as critical to the child's acceptance and adjustment to his handicap. In ways which are most often unconscious, parents are involved in the creation of their child's formative experience. This book alerts parents to the subtle influences which they exert over their children and the importance of coping with children who are handicapped.

Hobbs, Nicholas. *The Futures of Children.* San Francisco: Jossey-Bass, 1974.
An excellent reference for the parent to use in contesting school system decisions or in helping set up programs for the handicapped. The philosophy is one of mainstreaming, while also providing special services to all types of children in need. The book discusses not only the handicapped child, but the economically deprived and "delinquent" child within the educational and treatment systems.

Hofmann, Ruth B. *How to Build Special Furniture for Handicapped Children.* Springfield, Ill.: Charles C. Thomas, 1974.
A book of how-to's in constructing nineteen pieces of special equipment for handicapped children.

Kozol, Jonathan. *Death at an Early Age.* New York: Bantam, 1970.
A popular book in the late sixties with lessons that we have yet to learn. Although the book is based on the author's experiences in a compensatory education program in the Boston public schools, it can be generalized to a wider range of problems of miseducation. It is emotional, hard-hitting, and in many instances still true.

Melton, David. *When Children Need Help.* New York: Crowell, 1972.
This is an up-to-date handbook for parents of children who have been diagnosed as brain-injured, mentally retarded, cerebral palsied, learning disabled, or as slow learners.

Patterson, George W. *Helping Your Handicapped Child.* Minneapolis: Augsburg Publishing House, 1975. (PB)
The book discusses concerns typically raised in rearing a handi-

capped child: the initial questions asked, the denial phase, the contribution religion can make. Although the text is somewhat heavy, the chapter discussing the needs of the child, planning for the future, and involving the total family in planning for the special child can be helpful.

Robinault, Isabel P. *Functional Aids for the Multiply Handicapped.* Hagerstown, Md.: Harper & Row, 1973.
A book of special equipment and equipment adaptation ideas in the areas of mobility, personal care, communication, and recreation. Each chapter contains cautions, general principles to follow, and sources of where the equipment is available.

Rosenthal, Robert and Jacobsen, Lenore. *Pygmalion in the Classroom.* New York: Holt, Rinehart & Winston, 1968.
This book presents an understandable account of one of the most important pieces of educational research on teacher expectancies. In the study teachers were told that, based on tests, some children in their class would make considerable progress during the year and that others wouldn't. As predicted, children who were expected to "bloom" did, regardless of their ability or previous performance, and children who were not predicted to "bloom" didn't, suggesting that teacher expectancies are an important factor in children's learning and achievement.

Silberman, Charles E. *Crisis in the Classroom.* New York: Random House, 1971. (PB)
This book is the report of the Carnegie Study Commission on Education. It was written for laymen and educators alike, but it is a lengthy analysis of all the facets of American education—primarily its problems.

Spock, Benjamin M. and Lerrigo, Marion O. *Caring for Your Disabled Child.* New York: Macmillan, 1965. (PB)
The authors explain the opportunities afforded the handicapped child and young adult in the areas of medicine, education, rehabilitation, vocational training, leisure time, and social-sexual opportunities. There is a section on dealing with special problems, such as prosthetic devices and appliances and toileting care of the incontinent person.

Wentworth, Elise H. *Listen to Your Heart: A Message to Parents of Handicapped Children.* Boston: Houghton Mifflin, 1974.
Written with the intention of helping parents to find courage and deal with their own self-doubt, this text deals with how parents can reestablish faith in their own capabilities as individuals and as parents. The book takes an overall look at the problems most parents must solve when they have a child who is handicapped.

BRAIN DAMAGED, HYPERACTIVE, EPILEPTIC, APHASIC, LEARNING DISABLED

Anderson, Camilla M. *Jan, My Brain-Damaged Daughter*. Portland Ore.: Durham Press, 1963.

A professional mother's account of her pregnancy, delivery, and the problems, fears, joys, and frustrations of rearing her brain damaged daughter. This is a personal documentation of what a child's disability can mean to the family.

Bittinger, Marvin L. ed. *Living with our Hyperactive Children: Parents' Own Stories*. New York: BPS Books, Inc., Two Continents Publishing Group, Ltd., 1977.

The book is written by the families of hyperactive children to describe what it means to live with such a child. They recall in detail day-to-day events, their innermost feelings, and their joys and satisfactions in the child's achievements.

Browning, Elizabeth. *I Can't See What You're Saying*. New York: Coward, McCann, & Geohegan, 1973.

As the mother of an aphasic child, the author describes the apathy and ignorance that children with aphasia and their families confront daily. Although the setting of the book is in England, the many helpful suggestions are equally applicable to other cultures.

Brutten, Milton. *Something's Wrong with My Child. A Parent's Book About Children with Learning Disabilities*. New York: Harcourt-Brace-Jovanovich, 1973.

The book suggests how parents can identify the learning disabled child, how to find sources of diagnosis and treatment, how to live with and help them at home, and how to assist them in preparing for successful adult lives. It is well written and clearly presented.

Chaney, Clara M., and Kephart, Newell C. *Motoric Aids to Perceptual Training*. Columbus, Ohio: Charles E. Merrill, 1968.

This book offers a clear description of activities aimed at treating specific perceptual-motor and learning disabilities in children. Presented one step at a time, it includes a theoretical base, evaluation of behavior, training activities, and programs for such children, as well as for brain damaged and mentally retarded youngsters. It is a good guidebook for parents.

Clarke, Louise. *Can't Read, Can't Write, Can't Talk Too Good Either: How to Recognize and Overcome Dyslexia in Your Child*. New York: Walker, 1973.

A personal document by the parent of a severely language disabled child, this book provides a guide for parents to help them recognize the danger signals which may foretell future language problems. It also provides a glimpse of the maze of available treatment methods.

Well written, it vividly portrays the frustration of the child and parents and the uphill battle needed to be waged to obtain services from the schools and community at large.

Cohen, Martin E. and Davidson, Barbara. *Bets Wishz Doc: A Dynamic Approach to Learning Disabilities*. New York: Penguin, 1975.
An excellent book written by a professional who deals with learning disabled children in an educational setting. It gives parents a good description of what goes on in the classroom, and how both teacher and student must learn from one another.

Cruickshank, William M. *The Brain-Injured Child in Home, School and Community*. Syracuse, New York: Syracuse University Press, 1967.
The author gives a clear, concise picture of the symptoms of brain damage and recommends specific diagnostic techniques and procedures and the disciplines needed to carry them out. He provides information on classroom and home techniques which have been proven effective in working with brain damaged children. Included is an extensive reading list as well as names and addresses of national, state, and local organizations whose primary concern is the brain-injured child.

―――. *Learning Disabilities in Home, School and Community*. New York: Syracuse University Press, 1977.
This a revision of *The Brain-Injured Child in Home, School and Community* by the same author. The book, however, is not a repeat of the first edition. The author has updated the terms of vocabulary and terminology, expanded on his theories on the nature of learning disabilities, and answered parental concerns on the use of medication to control the behavior of these children.

Gardner, Richard. A. *MBD, The Family Book About Minimal Brain Dysfunction*. New York: Jason Aronson, 1973.
Part one of the book provides parents of children who are minimally brain damaged needed information about the problem of minimal brain dysfunction and what it means. The second half of the book is written for the child himself. It explains the condition, its effects on his behavior, and future expectations. The section is simply written and makes wide use of illustrations for the benefit of the child.

Lagos, Jorge C. *Seizures, Epilepsy and Your Child: A Handbook for Parents, Teachers, and Epileptics of All Ages*. New York: Harper & Row, 1974.
The author provides a practical guide to the nature, origins, diagnosis, treatment, and management of epilepsy. He attempts to answer questions involving the disorder which parents, teachers, acquaintances, or adults with epilepsy have. Included are listings of drugs used in treatment and their possible side effects. There is a very descriptive outline of milestones of psychomotor development.

Schoonover, Robert J. *Handbook for Parents of Children with Learning Disabilities*. Danville, Ill: Interstate Printers & Publishers, 1976. (PB)
An excellent guide for parents, this book details the meaning and behavioral symptoms of learning difficulties. Nearly half the book consists of practical activities to be used in the home for developing language, time and space concepts, mathematics, memory, and motor coordination.

Stewart, Mark A. and Olds, Sally W. *Raising a Hyperactive Child*. New York: Harper & Row, 1973.
This book explains the nature of problems presented by hyperactive children and describes practical ways to deal with them. It was written to give parents information about hyperactivity and to restore confidence in their ability to handle their child in a positive manner.

Wender, Paul W. *The Hyperactive Child*. New York: Crown Publishers, 1973.
This book is a guide for parents of hyperactive children and provides needed information about the problem of hyperactivity, its nature, causes, and treatment.

CEREBRAL PALSIED AND PHYSICALLY IMPAIRED

Denhoff, Eric. *Cerebral Palsy—The Preschool Years*. Springfield, Ill.: Charles Thomas, 1967.
An overview of the syndromes of cerebral dysfunction, its diagnosis, and its treatment in the early childhood years.

Finnie, Nancie. *Handling the Young Cerebral Palsied Child at Home*. New York: E. P. Dutton, 1975. (PB)
An excellent guide written to inform parents of the types of cerebral palsy, the influence of the disorder on the various aspects of the child's development, and specific techniques for dealing with the handicap. By far the major purpose of the book is to describe, with some detail, the numerous treatment and handling techniques for self-care, motor, and language development. The book also describes very practical equipment aids which can be made or modified in the home and lists resources for purchasing special equipment, such as strollers, chairs, potty seats, nipples, and feeding accessories.

Galbreaith, Patricia. *Hints for the Handicapped*. New York: Drake Publishers, 1974.
This book relates information about new and adaptive methods which facilitate independence for the physically handicapped. Included are ways to improve surroundings, increase interests or hobbies, encourage travel, manage children and household duties, and achieve self-care.

Griswold, P. A. *Play Together, Parents and Babies*. New York: United Cerebral Palsy, Inc., 1972. (PB)

A manual of activities for parents to use with their cerebral palsied child during play.

Joel, Gil S. *So Your Child Has Cerebral Palsy*. Albuquerque: University of New Mexico Press, 1975.

This book was written for parents by an individual who has cerebral palsy. It deals with many major questions and problems that are bound to arise in the family: the importance of early and exact diagnosis; the different types of treatment and rehabilitation; the relation between independence and self-sufficiency; the pitfalls of sheltered workshops and rehabilitation centers; home vs. residential care; and the more personal questions of affection, sex, and marriage. It is well written in an honest and straightforward manner. Although written specifically for the parents of the cerebral palsied child, any parent of a child with special needs will find it valuable.

Killilea, Marie. *Karen*. New York: Dell, 1968. (PB)

This is a true story of a child born with cerebral palsy who is helped by the patience, love, work, and faith of her family.

Murray, John B. *And Say What He Is: The Life of a Special Child*. Cambridge, Mass.: M.I.T. Press, 1975.

The book records one parent's diary of life with his cerebral palsied child from birth and diagnosis to death at the age of six.

EMOTIONALLY IMPAIRED

Axline, Virginia M. *Play Therapy*. New York: Ballantine Books, 1974. (PB)

Employing case material from a number of four- to twelve-year-old disturbed youngsters, this author practically illustrates how therapy can be incorporated into a child's play. Ms. Axline vividly describes a child's world as seen in play: his fears, angers, sadness, and love.

————. *Dibs: In Search of Self*. Westminister, Md.: Ballantine Books, 1976. (PB)

This book tells the story of a young boy's psychological battle for identity, which he accomplishes successfully with the help of play therapy. The book is interesting reading for those concerned with young children having emotional problems. The story is easy to read and clear in its description of the child's experiences.

Greenfeld, Josh, *A Child Called Noah: A Family Journey*. New York: Warner Books, 1973. (PB)

The author uses journal-type entries to describe an autistic child and his family. He details the anguish, elation, and depression which the family experiences as they raise this exceptional child.

Strauss, Susan. *Is It Well with the Child? A Parent's Guide to Raising Mentally Handicapped Children*. Garden City, N.Y.: Doubleday, 1975.

Written by a parent of an autistic child, this book relates the early suspicions and frustrations experienced by one family of a handicapped child. Well told, it deals largely with the impact of Michael on the family and the difficult decision to place him in a residential school.

HEARING IMPAIRED

Alpiner, Jerome G.; Amon, Carol F.; Gibson, Joy C.; and Sheehy, Patti. *Talk to Me.* 2 Volumes. Baltimore: Williams & Wilkins, 1977.
> The program is designed for use by parents, under the supervision of a clinician, of hearing impaired children from one to three years of age. The first volume contains parent/child activities; the second charts growth and development, including three-month progress reports.

Changing Sounds. Ears to Hear. Rules of Talking. Bill Wilkerson Hearing and Speech Center, 1114 19th Ave. S., Nashville, Tenn. 37212.
> These three pamphlets, and others written and distributed by the Wilkerson Center, are written specifically for parents of hearing impaired children. They are concerned with troubleshooting hearing aid problems, daily care and monitoring of aids, and natural language stimulation by parents on a daily basis. Reprints of articles are also available through the Center.

Katz, Lee; Mathis, S. L., III; and Merrill, E. C., Jr. *The Deaf Child in the Public Schools.* Danville, Ill. Interstate Printers & Publishers, 1974.
> This book offers a ready reference to parents who want their children to have a good educational experience, progressing to the full extent of their abilities in spite of hearing impairment. Written in a question and answer format, it is intended for parents of deaf children who are now attending, or may later attend, a public school. An extensive service agency listing and billiography are included.

Pollack, Doreen. *Educational Audiology for the Limited Hearing Infant.* Springfield, Ill.: Charles C. Thomas, 1975.
> The book outlines the acoupedic approach which involves auditory training without any other sensory cues for the infant and young child. The book is very helpful, but the approach should only be used with the supervision of trained therapists.

The Signed English Dictionary. Bornstein, Harry; Hamilton, Lillian B.; Saulnier, Karen Luczak; and Roy, Howard L., eds. Washington, D.C.: Gallaudet College Press, 1975.
> This is an easily read dictionary with good illustrations for about 2200 words in the Manual Signed English System. The words chosen represent the language level of preschool and elementary children. The dictionary could easily be used by parents with minimal assistance from therapists.

Signed English Series. Preschool Signed English Project. Washington, D.C.:
Gallaudet College, 1972–1975. (PB)
This series was designed for preschool and elementary hearing im-
paired/deaf children. It is thus far the best attempt to retain linguistic
integrity in a manual signal system. The small books are geared to the
younger child's cognitive and interest level and include some of the
old favorites like "The Three Little Pigs," as well as original preschool
stories.

MENTALLY RETARDED

Attwell, Arthur A. and Clabby, B. M. *The Retarded Child: Answers to Questions Parents Ask*. Los Angeles: Western Psychological Services, 1971.
A well-written guide which examines the causes, indentification, and
implications of mental retardation. Topics include family adjustment,
schooling, institutionalization, medical considerations, and parent
organizations on state and local levels.

Baldwin, Victor L. *Isn't It Time He Outgrew This? Or, Training Program for
Parents of Retarded Children*. Springfield, Ill.: Charles C. Thomas, 1973.
Behavior in a handicapped child is essentially the same as that of all
children, with undesirable behavior being a learned, not an un-
changeable manifestation of his handicap. Moving from this premise,
the author puts forth an easily understood program designed to
enable parents to assess needs, alter behavior, and evaluate the
progress achieved.

Blodgett, Harriett E. *Mentally Retarded Children: What Parents and Others
Should Know*. Minneapolis: University of Minnesota Press, 1971.
The book gives parents a framework of basic information concerning
mental retardation which will allow them to view the retarded individual realistically. The wide IQ range implied in the term *mental
retardation* is emphasized to reinforce that each retarded individual
needs to be seen in light of his own past and present levels of
functioning.

Canning, Claire D. *The Gift of Martha*. Boston: Children's Hospital Medical
Center Developmental Evaluation Clinic, 1975. (PB)
This book describes a family's reaction to the birth of a retarded child.
It emphasizes the emotional adjustment which needed to be made
before the child could become acceptable to the family.

Carlson, Bernice and Gingeland, David R. *Play Activities for the Retarded
Child*. New York: Abingdon Press, 1961.
This book is filled with games and activities designed to involve and
stimulate the physical, social, and mental growth of the retarded
child. Designed mainly for the home environment, it relies on parental initiation and reinforcement of interactions.

Dickerson, Martha Ufford. *Fostering Children with Mental Retardation.* Ypsilanti: Eastern Michigan University, 1977.

Two manuals (instructor and student) were developed to be used in sixteen training sessions to teach positive foster parenting for the child with mental retardation. Chapters include: Facts About Mental Retardation; Home Sweet Home; Positive Parenting; Getting to Know Your Foster Child; Learning the Specifics of Behavior; Introduction to Behavior Management; Assessing Behavior; and Focusing on Developmental Needs.

French, Edward L. and Scott, J. Clifford. *How You Can Help Your Retarded Child: A Manual for Parents.* Philadelphia: J. B. Lippincott, 1967.

The authors discuss simply and concisely the causes and types of retardation, how they are diagnosed, the relevance of intelligence quotient and social maturity tests, the special needs of the retarded, and the problems parents face in filling or coping with those needs. The emotional needs of both the child and parents are considered with suggestions for training and listings of special schools designed to provide services for the retarded.

Friedman, Paul K. *The Rights of Mentally Retarded Persons.* New York: Avon Books, 1976. (PB)

This book is an excellent guide for the parent of a retarded person of any age. The author describes guardianship and the rights of the retarded in institutions and in the criminal process. One chapter details the retarded person's legal right to an advocate.

Heard, J. Norman. *Hope Through Doing.* New York: John Day, 1968.

This is a story of one mentally retarded child as told by his father. Simply told, it examines the diagnostic period and the difficulties the family experienced in obtaining services for their child.

Isaacson, Robert. *The Retarded Child: A Guide for Parents and Friends.* Niles, Ill.: Argus Communications, 1974. (PB)

One of the best books written for a parent audience, this book deals with negative and positive feelings, parents' experience, and the pros and cons of major issues (e.g., institutionalization, financial help). The author describes handicapping conditions and their implications. One chapter is especially outstanding as it deals with communication between the marriage partners about the complexities of raising a handicapped child. A chapter on educational and vocational resources available completes this versatile parent guide.

Johnson, Vicki M. and Werner, Roberta A. *A Step-By-Step Learning Guide for Retarded Infants and Children.* Syracuse, New York: Syracuse University Press, 1975.

A programmed guide for teaching developmental skills to children with retardation who are developmentally less than two years old.

The guide gives specific information on behavior controls and motivation, as well as ordered tasks, specific objectives, and activities for sensory stimulation, social behavior, imitation, gross and fine motor skills, self-care, language, and perception.

_____. *A Step-By-Step Learning Guide for Older Retarded Children*. Syracuse, New York: Syracuse University Press, 1977.
A programmed guide designed for parents and teachers to be used with older children with retardation. The guide includes sections on effective teaching, behavior management, and developmental skill areas of self-care, gross and fine motor skills, language, and perception. Each section consists of a series of ordered tasks, objectives, and task implementation.

Kirk, Samuel A.; Karnes, Merle B.; and Kirk, Winifred D. *You and Your Retarded Child: A Manual for Parents of Retarded Children*. Palo Alto, Cal.: Pacific Books, 1968.
This book defines retardation and degrees of retardation and offers some help to parents through an extensive listing of normal behavior patterns at various stages of development, from three months to seven years of age. Issues such as placement and options for total programming (workshop, activity centers, etc.) are discussed. The bulk of the book deals with suggestions to parents for structuring their lifestyles and interactions so as to maximize the child's self-help skills, independence, and learning through play, speech, and social development. The chapter on discipline is practical and applicable to most family environments.

Lalor, Thomas. F. *Tom Tom*. New York: Harper & Row, 1973.
This book relates the story of a mentally retarded child as seen through the eyes of his father. Told simply, it deals with Tom's early diagnosis and the educational placement and later services needed for the child.

Larsen, Lawrence A., and Bricker, William A. *A Manual for Parents and Teachers of Severely and Moderately Retarded Children*. Nashville, Tenn.: Peabody College, 1968. (PB)
The book stresses that many behaviors exhibited by severely and moderately retarded children are learned and not just resultants of the child's mental retardation. Since behaviors have been learned, they can be unlearned and new behaviors taught. This manual provides a highly structured behavioral management program, which has been used effectively with severely and moderately retarded children.

Perske, Robert and Perske, Martha. *New Directions for Parents of Persons Who Are Retarded*. New York: Abingdon Press, 1973. (PB)
This is a good book for parents, with sketches of retarded children from childhood to adulthood. It is divided into four sections, includ-

ing focus on the parent, on the child, on the family, and on society. It is most helpful to parents who elect to keep their child in their home during puberty and the young adult years.

Roberts, Nancy. *David*. Richmond, Va.: John Knox Press, 1974. (PB)
This is written for parents by a parent. It contains beautiful pictures taken by David's father, a simple text discussing the diagnosis of Down's syndrome at birth, and a discussion of how the family grew to accept David as his personality developed and his skills changed. There are a lot of questions asked in the book, such as "why" and "what now." Most of them are answered in terms of parent advocacy. The book promotes parents as the prime movers of change.

————. *You and Your Retarded Child*. St. Louis: Concordia Publishing House, 1974. (PB)
Written by the parents of a Down's syndrome child, this book describes the initial trauma of learning about the child's handicap. It leads the reader through questions regarding what the future holds, the effect on the family, what the church can offer, and the problem of institutionalization. The book is strongly influenced by the authors' religious beliefs.

Schultz, Edna Moore. *Kathy*. Chicago: Moody Bible Institute, 1972. (PB)
Written by her mother, this book is a "biography" of a Down's syndrome girl—her birth, life, and death. It is written by a woman who learned to cope with her handicapped child through her religious convictions.

Smith, David W., and Wilson, Ann C. *The Child with Down's Syndrome*. Philadelphia: W. B. Saunders, 1973. (PB)
The authors discuss the genetic, physical, and medical aspects of Down's syndrome in some detail. One lengthy chapter pictorially portrays Down's syndrome infants, children, teens, and adults in daily life activities. The final chapter features statements by parents which describe the adjustments and plans they made for their special child.

Stephens, Beth, ed. *Training the Developmentally Young*. New York: John Day, 1971.
The book was written for teachers and therapists but can be helpful to knowledgeable parents. The reader is given a description of the trainable mentally retarded child and his capabilities. Included are cognitive, motor, language, and social developmental assessments; training techniques for perceptual-motor, speech and language, self-help, independence, recreation, and vocational skills; and an overview of Montessori technique, behavior modification, and discrimination learning.

Stout, Lucille. *I Reclaimed My Child*. Philadelphia: Chilton Books, 1959.

The book focuses on a family who initially institutionalized their Down's syndrome child. After gaining insight into the syndrome and learning about retardation, they reclaimed the child. The story shares with the reader the family and home adjustments after the child returned home.

Thornley, Margo L. *Every Child Can Learn . . . Something!* Seattle: Special Child, 1973.

This book provides an excellent guide to working with the severely involved child and teaching mentally retarded children.

Vulpe, Shirley G. *Home Care and Management of the Mentally Retarded Child.* Toronto, Ontario: National Institute on Mental Retardation of the Canadian Association of the Mentally Retarded, 1969. New volume expected soon.

This manual describes a wide array of flexible models for home care management. Its descriptive approach allows the models to be easily implemented by parents.

VISUALLY IMPAIRED

Halliday, Carol. *The Visually Impaired Child: Growth, Learning, Development: Infancy to School Age.* Louisville, Ky.: American Printing House for the Blind, 1971.

This book was written to be of practical value in the home care, training, and instruction of the visually impaired infant and preschool child. It outlines normal growth and development during the early years and provides suggestions for aiding the visually impaired child in meeting these milestones.

Krents, Harold. *To Race the Wind.* New York: Bantam, 1973. (PB)

This is an autobiography of a man who was blind from the age of eight. At that age, he and his parents refused to relegate him to the world of the blind. With courage and determination, the author overcame his fears, frustrations, loneliness, and the harassments and cruelties that people can exhibit. He went on to excel in high school, graduate from Harvard Law School, and study at Oxford.

Lowenfeld, Berthold. *Our Blind Children.* Springfield, Ill.: Charles C. Thomas, 1971.

A book written specifically for parents whose children are blind, the book includes chapters with explanations of and activities for developing physical and emotional independence, explanations of educational methods, and answers to questions parents ask most often.

Spencer, Marietta B. *Blind Children in the Family and Community.* Minneapolis: University of Minnesota Press, 1960.

The author shows how families can assist blind children to become useful, independent adults.

Superintendent of Public Instruction. *Preschool Learning Activities for the Visually Impaired Child: A Guide for Parents*. Springfield, Ill.: Office of Superintendent of Public Instruction, 1972.
This text provides a listing of games and activities to promote interaction with the environment. Also included is a list of agencies which offer services to blind children and their parents, and a suggested list of books for future reference.

Ulrich, Sharon. *Elizabeth*. Ann Arbor, Mi: University of Michigan Press, 1972.
A mother's well written and perceptive account of what it's like to raise a child who is blind.

Growth and Development
Barnard, P. E.; Demery, M.; Dickerson, M.; Kambouris, A.; and Lynch, E. *You and Me*. Detroit: Wayne County Intermediate School District, 1976. (PB) Free from Michigan Department of Education or Michigan local and intermediate school districts.
This booklet assists parents in understanding child development so they can recognize problems at an early age, know when to seek help, and know where to find needed resources. It is geared towards support for the parent in the child rearing role. The narrative is well written and informative and the accompanying photos are delightful.

Brazelton, T. Berry. *Infants and Mothers: Individual Differences in Development*. New York: Dell, 1969. (PB)
Dr. Brazelton traces normal growth and development in the young child. He illustrates the contrast among the very active, the moderately active, and the quiet baby to reveal the wide range of variations possible in normal growth and development. The need of the new mother to find her own way with her baby is stressed, as are the various mothering styles.

Crook, William G., M.D. *Can Your Child Read? Is He Hyperactive?* Jackson, Tenn.: Pedicenter Press, 1975. (PB)
Dr. Crook deals with the relationship of food allergies to hyperactivity, emotional behavior, and learning problems in children. The book provides detailed signs and symptoms signaling allergies and possible hyperactivity which parents can observe in their child. An extensive bibliography is included which documents the relationship of allergies to behavior and learning problems.

Elkind, David. *A Sympathetic Understanding of the Child: Birth to Sixteen*. Boston: Allyn & Bacon, 1974.
This book is a brief and easily read discussion of the major aspects of

child development. The author explains mental and social development through various stages with clear examples.

Fraiberg, Selma H. *The Magic Years*. New York: Charles Scribner's Sons, 1968. (PB)
This is a warmly written book showing how confusing and frightening the world of a child can be. Ms. Fraiberg perceptively discusses parental qualities that help the child to master developmental crises constructively. The book clearly and practically explains development, using an emotional-developmental base.

Gesell, Arnold, et. al., eds. *Infant and Child in the Culture of Today: The Guidance of Development in Home and Nursery School*. New York: Harper & Row, 1974.
Focusing on child growth characteristics, this book outlines specific, effective techniques for social and emotional guidance. Included are discussions of the relationship of the child to his environment, the development of individuality, and the significance of cultural differences. There are listings of suggested toys and equipment, books for children, and selected readings for adults.

Illingworth, R. S. *The Development of the Infant and Young Child*. Edinburgh: Churchill-Longman-Livingstone, 1976.
This book gives a clear description of the normal development of the infant and young child, as well as variations from the normal, to establish a basis for evaluating abnormal development. Although written primarily for pediatricians, some parents will also find the book of interest in explaining the necessity of the medical history, current diagnostic procedures, and an explanation of evaluation results.

Isaacs, Susan. *The Nursery Years: The Mind of the Child from Birth to Six Years*. New York: Schocken Books, 1968.
Ms. Isaacs deals with the developing child from birth to age six. The interdependency of the child's emotional, mental, affective, and language development during this period is emphasized. This short book is well written and provides some valuable insights into the nursery-aged child.

Leach, Penelope. *Babyhood*. New York: Alfred A. Knopf, 1976.
This book is a comprehensive and sometimes technical guide written for parents. It describes what a baby and toddler will do, rather than what the parent should do. The book is divided into five sections: the first six weeks, from six weeks to three months, from three to six months, from six to twelve months, and the second year. Within each section, Dr. Leach describes the baby's physical, emotional, and mental development.

Princeton Center for Infancy and Early Childhood. *The First Twelve Months of Life: Your Baby's Growth Month by Month*. New York: Grosset & Dunlap, 1973. (PB)

With beautiful photographs, this book describes, month-by-month, the world of the infant to twelve-month-old child. It discusses development in motor, language, mental, and social realms, and provides parents with a clear understanding of growth in the first year.

Schrieber, Flora R. *Your Child's Speech*. New York: Ballantine Books, 1973. (PB)

The first section of this book deals with normal language from birth to the early school years, in a developmental framework. The second section deals with handicapping conditions which influence this development (such as mental retardation, deafness, cerebral palsy), symptoms for recognizing language deviations, and some recommendations for treatment. The third section discusses specific speech handicaps, such as poor articulation and stuttering. Although applicable to most handicaps, the book's recommendations for the retarded child are not complete.

White, Burton L. *The First Three Years of Life*. Englewood Cliffs, N.J.: Prentice-Hall, 1975.

The author recommends techniques conducive to the educational development at each stage of the child's physical, cognitive, and social growth.

Parenting

Abrahamson, David. *The Emotional Care of Your Child*. Berkeley: Trident Press, 1969.

In this book a psychoanalyst, writing specifically for parents, discusses techniques for adjusting and resolving conflicts which arise while bringing up a child. It is a helpful book designed to aid parents in recognizing mistakes and remedying them before additional problems are created.

Adler, Manfred. *A Parents' Manual:. Answers to Questions on Child Development and Child Rearing*. Springfield, Ill.: Charles C. Thomas, 1971.

This book answers frequently asked questions on child development and child rearing. It is intended as a guide—a beginning point for interested parents.

Arnstein, Helene S. *What to Tell Your Child about Birth, Death, Illness, Divorce, and Other Family Crises*. New York: Bobbs-Merrill, 1964. (PB)

This book deals with possible crises a family might experience and how to handle the situations with children. Topics covered include family financial problems, remarriage, hospitalization of the parent or child, and when mother goes back to work. The author attempts to stimulate creative thinking in approaching and handling family crises. Bibliographies are also included for further reading.

Becker, Wesley C. *Parents Are Teachers: A Child Management Program.* Champaign, Ill.: Research Press, 1971.
This is a programmed text to give parents a workable knowledge of behavior management. The book deals with how parents can consciously use consequences to teach their children and change behavior in positive and reinforcing ways. Illustrative examples are used widely throughout the text.

Bel Geddes, Joan. *How To Parent Alone.* New York: Seabury Press, 1974.
The book is written for the parent who becomes single through divorce or death. It is based on the theory that people have resources within that allow them to profit from and enjoy single parenthood. It should be read by all parents as preparatory to the unknown.

Biklen, Douglas. *Let Our Children Go.* Syracuse, New York: Human Policy Press, 1974. (PB)
This book is written for parents who question the current system for the delivery of services to their handicapped children. It is intended to help parents organize as advocates to bring about change.

Bowley, Agatha H. *Children at Risk.* New York: Churchill-Livingstone, 1975. (PB)
The author shares with the reader some of her experiences in working with children at risk and their parents. Emphasized is that parents, teachers, and other professionals should provide children with basic needs, security, love, care, and guidance so that the child may develop into a mature, adjusted, creatively constructive, and uniquely valued individual.

Braga, Laurie. *Learning and Growing: A Guide to Child Development.* Englewood Cliffs, N.J.: Prentice-Hall, 1975.
The book explains how children learn from doing and experiencing while growing. The author has selected behaviors which typify children of specific age ranges and suggests ways to manage unwanted behaviors. Also included are stimulation activities for each age range.

Child Study Association of America. *What to Tell Your Child About Sex.* New York: Jason Aronson, 1974.
What to Tell Your Child About Sex is an easy to read book which discusses various questions children are likely to ask about sex. Children's different age levels are taken into consideration. There are illustrations parents can use with their children and reading suggestions for parents, children, and young people.

Dickerson, Martha Ufford. *Fostering Children with Mental Retardation.* Ypsilanti: Eastern Michigan University, 1977.
Two manuals (instructor and student) were developed to be used in sixteen training sessions to teach positive foster parenting for the child with mental retardation. Some of the chapters are: Facts About Mental Retardation; Home Sweet Home; Positive Parenting; Getting

to Know your Foster Child; Learning the Specifics of Behavior; Introduction to Behavior Management; Assessing Behavior; Focusing on Developmental Needs.

Division of Child Behavior and Development, Wisconsin State Board of Health. *Talks with Parents*. Madison, Wisconsin. (PB)
The book attempts to recognize some of the many questions that parents of children may ask. It provides no judgmental answers but guides the parents in thinking about the experiences they have had with their children, what the experiences represent, and how to cope with mixed feelings and pressures from society.

Dodson, Fitzhugh. *How to Father*. Los Angeles: New American Library, 1974. (PB)
The author attempts to help fathers recognize specific needs that their children may have and suggests how a father can best fulfill those needs by stepping beyond his traditional role.

————. *How to Parent*. New York: New American Library, 1973. (PB)
Giving birth to a child does not automatically make one a wise or effective parent. To do a really good job, it is essential to know a great deal about the way children grow. Dr. Dodson tells the reader what to expect during the different stages leading to maturity and how to use this knowledge most effectively to meet and deal with the behaviors which occur. Appendices include toys and play equipment for different ages, free and inexpensive stimulating toys, a guide to children's books and records, and a bibliography of additional books on parenting.

Dreikurs, Rudolf and Soltz, Vicki. *Children: The Challenge*. New York: Hawthorne, 1976. (PB)
Through the use of case studies the author has organized, in an easy to follow form, specific situations and challenges that parents have encountered with their children. Each situation is followed by appropriate, tested solutions and the reasoning and principles behind the solutions.

Ginott, Haim G. *Between Parent and Child*. New York: Macmillan, 1965.
Ginott's purpose is to aid parents in devising manageable goals and successful methods for child rearing. He confronts common situations and offers suggestions in a practical manner. Emphasis is placed on communication with children and the acceptance of them as individuals.

Gordon, Ira J. *The Infant Experience*. Columbus, Ohio: Charles E. Merrill, 1975. (PB)
This book emphasizes the phenomenon of infancy and the influences upon it (physiology, culture, parent-child interaction). Although written as a report on the results of the Florida Infant Project, this

book is useful to parents interested in learning how their culture and interactions affect their child's development. The book also describes how a child's competency and parent's skills are developed within a variety of cultural environments.

Gordon, Thomas. *Parent Effectiveness Training: The Tested New Way to Raise Responsible Children.* New York: New American Library, 1975. (PB)
This book provides parents with an understanding of effective parent-child interaction. Practical areas of concern are discussed, such as accepting, listening, structuring the environment to prevent behavior problems, dealing with conflicts, and assisting parental surrogates to function in the best interest of the child.

Grollman, Earl A. *Talking About Death—A Dialogue Between Parent and Child with Parent's Guide & Recommended Resources.* Boston: Beacon Press, 1976.
Talking About Death presents a sensitive dialogue between a parent and child on death. A "Parent Guide" to the dialogue helps parents to use the model when discussing a loved one's death with a child, as well as helping themselves deal with the sorrow of death. The book also contains an annotated listing of resources, such as services, films, organizations, and books for further use.

Harrison-Ross, Phyllis, M.D. and Wyden, Barbara. *The Black Child—A Parent's Guide.* New York: Peter H. Wyden, 1973.
This book is geared toward helping the parents and teachers of black children to provide necessary stimulation and guidance. It discusses the problems of being black, growing up in a white world, and offers insight into racial differences.

Honig, Alice S. *Parent Involvement in Early Childhood Education.* Washington, D.C.: National Association for the Education of Young Children, 1975. (PB)
This book focuses on parents as active participants in early child development and education program models. The positive over-comings and negative barriers encountered in parent involvement are discussed with specific suggestions to assist parents.

Horrobin, J. Margaret, and Rynders, John E. *To Give an Edge.* Minneapolis: Colwell Press, 1975. (PB)
A well-written guide for parents of Down's syndrome children, this book describes the day-to-day care and development of the child. The book includes a discussion of training and play activities. It is realistic but optimistic.

Jones, Sandy. *Good Things for Babies.* Boston: Houghton Mifflin, 1976. (PB)
This is an excellent catalog of clothing, toys, and other essentials which have been recommended for the consumers of baby products. Included with the majority of entries are costs, descriptions, and

where the item may be purchased. (Some illustrations are included.)

Lynn, David B. *The Father: His Role in Child Development.* Monterey, Cal.: Brooks/Cole, 1974.

The author encompasses many problems related to father-child relationships. Focus is placed on the cultural determinants of fathering coupled with the changing roles in today's society, marital and parental patternings, and socioeconomic status. The author also discusses different theories concerning the role of a father, the father-mother relationship, and the identification of sex roles.

Markun, Patricia Maloney, ed. *Parenting.* Washington, D.C.: The Association for Childhood Education International, 1973. (PB)

The book attempts to assist parents in dealing and coping with raising children. Responsibility for child development is given to the parent first, and the significance of this relationship on the child's future social-psychological functioning is discussed. A distinction is made between parenting and parenthood; stress is placed on parents serving as builders and maintainers of their child's mental growth and development.

Patterson, Gerald R., and Gullion, M. Elizabeth. *Living With Children: New Methods for Parents and Teachers.* Eugene, Oregon: Research Press, 1976. (PB)

This book is a programmed text designed to show parents how to encourage desirable behaviors in their children and gradually eliminate unwanted behaviors. The theoretic base is that all behavior is learned.

Reich, Hanns, ed. *Children and Their Fathers.* New York: Hell and Wang, 1962.

This is a pictorial book which shares with the reader the friendships and enjoyments which fathers and their children can have with one another.

Smith, Helen Wheeler. *Survival Handbook for Preschool Mothers.* Chicago: Follett, 1977.

This book is a guide on what to expect as a parent and how to deal with the child in a positive and mutually reinforcing manner. It also includes suggested activities to promote parent-child interactions and foster intellectual growth of the young child.

Staff of the Prevention of Speech and Language Handicaps Project. *Partners in Language.* Washington: American Speech and Hearing Association, 1973. (PB)

Written in English and Spanish, this book uses simple language and illustrations to emphasize the importance that parent-child interactions have on early language development. Daily life routines are emphasized as enhancing the child's development through interaction with his care-givers (bathtime, mealtime, rides in the car, simple games).

Wolf, Anna. *The Parent's Manual: A Guide to the Emotional Development of Young Children*, 2nd ed. New York: Simon & Schuster, 1962.
The author describes realistically what it is like to bring home a new baby and what can be expected from the newborn's siblings. She gives guidance to parents on discipline, peer relationships, and sexuality in childhood. Problems of parenting and the concept of the forgotten father are also addressed. Included are suggestions of things to make and do with young children.

Play and Stimulation Activities

Arena, John I., ed. *Teaching Through Sensory-Motor Experiences*. San Rafael, Cal.: Academic Therapy Publications, 1969. (PB)
This book includes a collection of articles dealing with topics such as body image and awareness, discrimination, and eye-hand coordination. Each contributor includes activities for fostering learning through experiences.

Baker, Katherine Read. *Let's Play Outdoors*. Washington, D.C.: National Association for the Education of Young Children, 1967.
This book contains many suggestions for outdoor activities. The author emphasizes the need for parents and teachers to maximize the abilities of their children by enhancing learning opportunities.

Behrmann, Polly. *Activities for Developing Auditory Perception*. San Rafael, Cal.: Academic Therapy Publications, 1975. (PB)
A manual of exercises designed to train and improve the many areas of auditory perception. Activities are simply explained and geared for children from kindergarten through the elementary grades, but they can be readily adapted for use with older children. All exercises are of short duration, easy, fun to do, and require a minimum of materials.

Behrmann, Polly, and Millman, Joan. *Experience for Children in Learning*. Cambridge, Mass.: Educators Publishing Service, 1968. (PB)
This book is a collection of simple children's activities that can be played at home, in the car, or outside. Besides being fun, they strengthen and develop the child's skills. All activities are easily accomplished with materials and means available in the home.

Blumenfeld, Jane; Thompson, Pearl; and Vogel, Beverly. *Help Them Grow: A Pictorial Handbook for Parents of Handicapped Children*. Nashville, Tenn.: Abingdon Press, 1971. (PB)
This book provides a basic structure for integrating the child into family life and gives basic suggestions for developing self-help, social, safety, communication, and sensory motor skills. The book might serve as a beginning reader for parents of mildly involved

preschoolers and elementary children, as it only touches the surface of many of the complexities of raising a handicapped child.

Braley, William T., et al. *Daily Sensorimotor Training Activities.* Freeport, N.Y.: Educational Activities, 1968.
Activities suggested are designed to be integrated into curriculums using specifically designed equipment. However, parents can very easily provide or facilitate the same experiences at home. Daily sensory and motor development activities are suggested, with specific goals designed to aid children in academic achievement. Its primary focus is to help children overcome sensorimotor deficits.

Brown, Sara, and Donovan, Carol. *Stimulation Activities. Vol. III of Developmental Programming for Infants and Young Children.* Edited by Schafer and Moersch. Ann Arbor: University of Michigan Press, 1977.
A book of suggested activities to meet specified goals, this book was designed to be used by parents of children from birth to three years of age under the supervision of professionals. The activities are divided into six areas: fine motor, gross motor, language, self-care, cognition, and social. Adaptations are given for sensory and motor handicaps.

Caney, Steven. *Play Book.* New York: Workman, 1975. (PB)
Becase play is a natural activity for children, it should not be confined to specific areas such as the playroom or the child's bedroom. The author feels that parents should make use of normal and everyday situations and incorporate them into the child's play or learning experiences. Included in the contents are over fifty suggestions for making the best use of areas such as the kitchen, porch, closet, garage, steps, yard, etc. to help children develop imagination, creative skills, and self-initiated play activities.

———. *Toy Book.* New York: Workman, 1972. (PB)
The author feels that children are better off with toys geared toward more than one learning experience. He suggests and provides simple directions for over fifty toys that a parent or teacher and child can make together, as a group, or individually. The materials for these toys are economical, as they are generally items which would have been discarded.

Cratty, Bryant. *Active Learning.* Englewood, N.J.: Prentice-Hall, 1970.
The author attempts to explain as simply as possible how active games can be used to facilitate the acquisition of academic skills. He offers specific suggestions as to methods and activities that deal with coordination deficits.

———. *Developmental Sequences of Perceptual-Motor Tasks, Movement Activities for Neurologically Handicapped and Retarded Children and Youth.* Freeport, N.Y.: Educational Activities, 1967.
The author provides evidence as to the significance of perceptual-

motor activities in the educational programming for retarded, as well as normal and neurologically handicapped children. Specific suggestions as to how parents and teachers can contribute to a child's experiences are included, with specific suggestions for program planning based on the disability of the child.

_____. *Intelligence in Action. Physical Activities for Enhancing Intellectual Abilities.* Engelwood Cliffs, N.J.: Prentice-Hall, 1973.
The book very tactfully illustrates how to use movement programs to enhance academic deficits in language skills, short term memory, and problem solving. The activities suggested are geared to assist in maximizing the ability of children to develop cognitive skills.

Drezek, Wendy, and Harmon, Mary Anne. *Parents and Children: Activities and Environments for Infants and Toddlers.* Austin, Tex.: Austin-Travis County Mental Health, Mental Retardation Center, 1976. (PB)
This booklet describes the influence of environment and care-giving attitudes and activities on the development of the child at four stages of development: birth through four months, five to eight months, nine to eighteen months, and nineteen to thirty months. The narrative is interesting and well-written, but the pictures tell the story of successful parent-child interaction.

Gordon, Ira J. *Baby Learning through Baby Play: A Parent's Guide for the First Two Years.* New York: St. Martin's Press, 1970. (PB)
This book is a simply written guide to games and activities that encourage growth in various areas of development. It is nicely illustrated.

Gordon, Ira; Guinagh, B.; and Jester, R. E. *Child Learning Through Child Play: Learning Activities for Two and Three Year Olds.* New York: St. Martin's Press, 1972. (PB)
This book provides learning activities for toddlers. It has some good suggestions for games that provide stimulation to promote mental growth and development.

Gregg, Elizabeth M., and Boston Children's Medical Center Staff. *What To Do When There's Nothing To Do.* New York: Dell, 1968. (PB)
Each chapter briefly discusses a phase of the infant's or young child's development and offers activities appropriate to the age level discussed (e.g., babies; toddlers and crawlers; two- and three-year olds; three-, four- and five-year-olds). Activities suggested can be melded into the daily routine, and much of the equipment suggested can be found in the average home. The appendix lists children's books and records.

Hatten, John T., and Hatten, Pequetti W. *Natural Language: A Clinician-guided Program for Parents of Language-delayed Children.* Revised edition. Tucson, Ariz.: Communication Skill Builders, 1975. (PB)

This book is written for parents, to be used in conjunction with the ongoing therapy of children who have acquired some language skills, but whose language is delayed to the point of parental concern. The book nicely interweaves sensory, cognitive, and motor development with the growth of language skills. Structured activities are described.

Jordan, June, and Dailey, Rebecca, eds. *Not All Wagons Are Red: The Exceptional Child's Early Years*. Arlington, Va.: The Council for Exceptional Children, 1973.

This book reflects the many approaches to early childhood education based on the Invisible Colleges' Conference on Early Childhood Education and the Exceptional Child. Emphasis is given to the rationale and historical perspective for early intervention and the identification of the high risk child or child with special needs. Suggestions are given as to appropriate programming for these children, available resources, how to maximize the use of professionals, how to train personnel, and methods to implement change.

Kahan, Ellen H. *Cooking Activities for the Retarded Child*. Nashville, Tenn.: Abingdon Press, 1974.

The book demonstrates ways in which retarded children can be given new skills, enabling them to become more independent in the kitchen. It provides a descriptive and functional technique for teaching the basic skills necessary for meal preparation, cooking, and cleaning up. A few simplified recipes are included.

Kier, Dell C. *The Significance of the Young Child's Motor Development*. Washington, D.C.: National Association for Education of Young Children, 1971. (PB)

Guidance is given to parents in understanding motor development and why development should be closely observed. Emphasis is on the need for children to experience gross and fine motor skills which enhance total body awareness, coordination, and movement.

Language Development Programs Staff. *Our World, Our Words*. Nashville, Tenn.: Bill Wilkerson Hearing and Speech Center, 1976. (PB)

These three volumes contain easily read directions for activities around the home, work in the home, and outside "adventures." They are fun to read; the illustrations are delightful.

Levy, Janine. *The Baby Exercise Book: For the First Fifteen Months*. New York: Pantheon Books, 1976. (PB)

This book is written to provide parents with ways of physically manipulating and stimulating their child to encourage his motor development and to increase positive play interactions between parent and child. The narrative is clearly written and photographs further explain the exercises. The exercises are most appropriate for the child whose developmental stage is between birth and walking independently.

Caution: This exercise book should not be used if the child is stiff, spastic, or difficult to relax.

Lucas, Virginia. *Classroom Activities for Helping Slower Learning Children.* West Nyack, N.Y.: The Center for Applied Research in Education, Inc., 1974. (PB)

This book provides activities and experiences for the slower learning child. Emphasis is placed on the individual child's unique learning style and on the need for the teacher or parent to provide models, repetition, and reinforcers for the learning situation.

Nickelsburg, Janet. *Nature Program for Early Childhood.* Reading, Mass.: Addison Wesley, 1976. (PB)

Forty-four nature projects are included to encourage children to stop, look, listen, and thus learn from their environment. They are also encouraged to experiment, develop an ability to express themselves, and make use of all their senses while observing. Each section provides helpful materials and background information to assist parents and teacher in maximizing the learning process.

Sharp, Evelyn. *Thinking Is Child's Play.* New York: Avon, 1970.

The first half of this book provides a survey of current research about children's thinking. This research is used in the second half to suggest a large number of games that may be played with children. It is based on the concept that playing games will provide parents with needed insights into how their children think and will contribute to children's own thinking processes.

Staff of Developmental Language and Speech Center. *Teach Your Child to Talk.* New York: CEBCD Standard Publishing Co. (PB)

This book deals with speech and language in a developmental framework between the ages of birth and five years. It is easy to read with attractive illustrations. There are activities at each age grouping suitable to the family's routine. A description of finger plays and a bibliography of books and records for children are an added bonus.

Caution: The book would not be appropriate for a severely involved child without ongoing help from a speech therapist.

Steiner, Violette, and Pond, Roberta. *Finger Play Fun.* Columbus, Ohio: Charles C. Merrill, 1970.

This book provides a collection of old and new finger plays designed especially to help children with language development.

Stock, Claudette. *Learning Activities.* Boulder, Colo.: Pruett, 1970.

This book describes sensory-motor activities which can enhance the development of children with learning deficits in their early years.

Upchurch, Beverly. *Easy To Do Toys and Activities for Infants and Toddlers*. Greensboro, N.C.: University of North Carolina, 1971.

Ideas, directions, and patterns are given for making appropriate toys from simple household materials. Each toy is described and geared to a particular age span; materials needed and directions to make the toy are given. A list of where materials are available and their approximate cost is also given.

Wilson, Sue. *I Can Do It! I Can Do It! Arts and Crafts for the Mentally Retarded*. Abilene, Tex.: Quality, 1976. (PB)

This excellent, well-illustrated book describes specific arts and crafts projects for a mentally retarded child functioning at any level. The materials are economical, and helpful. Precautions are given on some projects, i.e., toxicity of some paints. Each project is labelled as to its therapeutic advantages, i.e., fine or gross motor skills, time estimations. The book has oversized print so that children may easily work independently.

Siblings

Blume, Judy. *Deenie*. New York: Dell, 1977. (PB)

The book is sensitively written for the junior high population. It tells the study of a girl with idiopathic scoliosis and the problems she had to face during the bracing period.

Brightman, Alan. *Like Me*. Boston: Little, Brown & Company, 1976. (PB)

This small, beautiful book with color photographs of all sizes, types, and shapes òf children points out that children are alike in many ways, even though some of them are slower than others. It appeals to children of all ages and the "personal note" at the end is highly recommended for both children and adults.

Clearly, Margaret. *Please Know Me As I Am: A Guide to Helping Children Understand the Child with Special Needs*. Sudbury, Pa.: Jerry Cleary, 1975. (PB)

Emphasis is placed on physical, mental, and emotional needs of children with developmental disabilities. It tries to increase normal children's awareness and consideration for those with special needs. Activities are suggested and a list of resource agencies is included within the text. It is appropriate for older elementary through junior high school students.

Fassler, Joan. *Howie Helps Himself*. Chicago: Albert Whitman & Co., 1975.

Though he enjoys life with his family and attends school, Howie, a child with cerebral palsy, wants more than anything else to be able to move his wheelchair by himself. This book is directed to older elementary and young junior high students.

————. *One Little Girl*. New York: Behavioral Publishers, 1969.

The author tells a simple story about a "slow" child and how the perspective of the child was influenced by the adults dealing with her and talking about her. It is an excellent book for preschoolers and early elementary children.

Gold, Phyllis. *Please Don't Say Hello*. New York: Human Sciences Press, 1975.
An excellent book for adolescent siblings of autistic children. In a narrative form, with many illustrations, the author shares with the reader a family's technique for facilitating acceptance of their autistic child by other children and their parents.

Huebener, Theodore. *Special Education Careers*. New York: Franklin Watts, 1977.
This book describes the various careers in special education and job opportunities in major U.S. cities for such occupations. It is an excellent source for a junior high and older student interested in special education fields.

Lasker, Joe. *He's My Brother*. Chicago: Albert Whitman & Co., 1974.
Written for siblings of "slow" or learning disabled children, this book describes simply, but realistically, the behaviors and need for understanding that such children have. It is most appropriate for elementary students.

LeShan, Eda. *Learning to Say Good-By*. New York: Macmillan, 1976.
This book discusses the questions and fears children experience when a parent or someone close to them dies. The book is written so it could be read by older elementary through high school students.

Levine, Edna S. *Lisa and Her Soundless World*. New York: Human Science Press, 1976.
A book which describes the physical and emotional problems of the hearing impaired, this book is excellent for older elementary and junior high students.

Luis, Earlene W., and Millar, Barbara F. *Listen, Lissa*. New York: Dodd, Mead, & Co., 1968.
This valuable book presents the problems and joys facing the family and friends of an eleven-year-old boy who is severely retarded. It is suitable for junior high and older children.

Ominsky, Elaine. *Jon O., A Special Boy*. Englewood Cliffs, N.J.: Prentice-Hall, 1977.
Ms. Ominsky guides the reader with words and pictures through the world of a Down's syndrome child. Written with a simple text, the book is intended as an introduction to what it is like to be different. The book is suitable for older elementary children.

Peterson, Jeanne Whitehouse. *I Have A Sister; My Sister Is Deaf*. New York: Harper & Row, 1977.
A beautiful story which stresses the abilities a deaf child has to

compensate for her hearing loss. It is appropriate for preschool and elementary children.

Sobol, Harriet Langsam. *Jeff's Hospital Book*. New York: Henry Z. Walck, 1975.
This book tells all about Jeff and how he feels when he is taken to the hospital to have an eye operation. It is an excellent book written to prepare preschoolers and early elementary children for the hospital experience. There are pictures of nurses, doctors, treatments, and the operating room.

———. *My Brother Steven Is Retarded*. New York: Macmillan, 1977.
This is an excellent, pictorial book which concentrates on the unique relationship between an adolescent girl and her retarded brother. Beth isn't sure how she feels about her brother, yet describes what it is like to be part of a family with a retarded child. She tells of the exciting good times and the cruel and embarrassing moments as well. A good book for junior high and high school students.

Stein, Sara B. *About Handicaps*. New York: Walker & Co., 1974.
A sensitive book which provides parents with illustrative examples of how to deal with ordinarily and extraordinarily difficult questions asked by their children. The book is recommended for ages three to eight.

Wolf, Bernard. *Don't Feel Sorry for Paul*. Philadelphia: Lippincott, 1974.
The book describes and illustrates a two week period in the life of a young handicapped boy, and how he lived successfully in a world made for people without handicaps. It is directed to junior high students.

Contributors

BROWN, SARA L. Speech and Language Therapist, Early Intervention Project; Coordinator, Early Invention Project—Outreach

D'EUGENIO, DIANE B. Occupational Therapist, Early Intervention Project and Early Intervention Project—Outreach

DICKERSON, MARTHA UFFORD Program Associate for Social Work, Institute for the Study of Mental Retardation and Related Disabilities (ISMRRD); Social Work Consultant, Early Intervention Project; Foster Parent

GRASS, LINDA R. Special Educator/Psychologist; Coordinator, Early Intervention Project—Outreach, 1976–77

HASKIN, SUZANNE Parent, Early Intervention Project; Project Associate, Early Intervention Project—Outreach

JAWOROWSKI, RON Parent, Early Intervention Project

JAWOROWSKI, SALLY Parent, Early Intervention Project

LYNCH, ELEANOR W. Program Director for Special Education, ISMRRD; Special Education Consultant, Early Intervention Project

McDONALD, GAY S. Special Educator, Early Intervention Project—Outreach

MEYER, JOAN YOUNG Parent

MOERSCH, MARTHA S.   Program Director for Occupational Therapy, ISMRRD; Project Director, Early Intervention Project and Early Intervention Project—Outreach

NELSON, VIRGINIA S.   Acting Program Director for Pediatrics, ISMRRD; Pediatric Consultant, Early Intervention Project

PETERSON, JANE   Parent, Early Intervention Project

PETERSON, LARRY   Parent, Early Intervention Project

ROGERS, SALLY J.   Assistant Professor of Psychology, Southwestern Missouri State University; Psychologist, Early Intervention Project

SEGAL, ROBERT M.   Program Director for Social Work, ISMRRD

VUKOVICH, PAULA   Parent, Early Intervention Project

WRIGHT, PAULINE L.   Occupational Therapist, Early Intervention Project – Outreach